contents

acting**characters**

20 simple steps from rehearsal to performance

The author would like to thank the following for their help with this book: Sarah Hughes, Sybil Eysenck, Jenny Ridout, Alan Ayckbourn, Ian Chappell, Gemma Albon, Katie Taylor, Hilary Lissenden.

For Chris, and for Mike and Amy

acting**characters**
20 simple steps from rehearsal to performance

paul elsam

a & c black • london

First published 2006

A & C Black Publishers Limited
38 Soho Square
London W1D 3HB
www.acblack.com

ISBN 0-7136-7586-1

A CIP catalogue record for this book is available from
the British Library.

Cover illustration by Joanna Nelson

Typeset in 10/13pt Plantin and
10.5/13pt MetaPlusNormal

Printed and bound in Great Britain by
Creative Print and Design (Wales), Ebbw Vale

foreword

There's a lot of nonsense written about acting, much of it by people who have never acted or spent any time with someone who does. It's good to welcome a practical, uncluttered book written by someone who has done both.

Similarly, writing as one who spent the first eight years of his working life pursuing a faltering acting career and the next 40 as a director trying to help others to do the job better, I feel I know a little about the subject.

I have, after all, spent years of my life in rehearsal rooms, day after day watching the acting process (and more importantly what leads up to the acting process), first hand. Sometimes this can be laborious (like watching paint dry); at other times, it's instinctively swift and near-miraculous, witnessing one personality melt into another.

Yet if that all sounds rather mystical, whatever route the actor takes towards a finished interpretation, in the right company, with the right fellow actors, text, director and the reassuring safety net of good technical support from the other departments, it's also enormous fun.

True, acting entails a great deal of patience, application and sheer hard work – make no mistake; and I know it is rather frowned upon to link hard work with fun, certainly in this country. But the two, surely, need not – should not – be mutually exclusive.

Acting is one of those extraordinary, sometimes frustrating jobs wherein the less of it you seem to be doing, the better you appear to be doing it.

As, I suspect, is true of most art. Many of the greatest achievements are produced joyously, as if guided by instinct. Likewise some of the dullest work is the result of painful grind and endless hard labour – and it shows. We may faintly applaud the obvious huge effort put into it all but nonetheless we soon turn away or leave at the interval.

So, aspiring actor-to-be who may be planning to read this book, always trust your instincts first and foremost. However good you are, they will be proven wrong once in a while – but as long as you don't get immovably entrenched, you can always retract later. And if your first instincts do prove unfailingly wrong more often than not, then perhaps you should start pursuing a different career, as I did.

Paul Elsam is a former actor who now teaches and directs. His approach is technical and refreshingly non-academic. He charts clear and helpful pathways to guide the student actor towards a performance, which can be very useful, believe me. In choosing to become a professional actor you are, in return for an often pitiful remuneration, contracted to produce something watchable and stageworthy within a finite time to perform over a finite period. Sometimes, long before rehearsals have finished or even started, people have already paid good money for their seats.

And no matter how good your instincts, in the end you will also need a surefire practical technique to fall back on. In this book, Paul quite rightly makes the point that good actors are well aware that it is not possible to be at the height of their game every night, eight times a week, month in month out. There will be days when 'inspiration' deserts them. Those are the days on which technique comes into play to compensate for this. And, if you get to be really good, most people will never tell the difference.

Sir Alan Ayckbourn
Scarborough 2005

introduction

What is your technique for creating a character? What, indeed, is a 'character'?

The very concept of the actor's character in drama is quite a controversial one. Since Stanislavski wrote *Building a Character* in the early 20th century, generations of actors have pursued the mercurial task of capturing the essence of their character. Yet playwright and director David Mamet among others asserts passionately that there is no such thing as a character, just an actor, whose simple task is to serve the play in the manner prescribed by the playwright.

Certainly there are traps for the actor who wants to be able to create a character. There is the seductive urge to make the character memorable and interesting, which can lead to all sorts of questionable character choices ranging from a slight stammer to a tendency to scratch without reason! There is the temptation to lead your character off in an emotional direction which feels artistically satisfying, but happens to run counter to the play. There is the simple danger that the more you delve into your own character, the less you may notice those around you.

Alan Ayckbourn tells the story of when he was a young actor rehearsing the role of Stanley in *The Birthday Party*, under the direction of playwright Harold Pinter. Keen to do a good job, Alan badgered Harold for nuggets of information about his character. Harold calmly told him to 'mind your own ****ing business'.

The bottom line is that the most interesting, spontaneous, responsive, and three-dimensional character you can harness is you. This is quite handy because if you basically play yourself, as some actors do, you can put all of your energy into responding truthfully to situations encountered in the play. It's common today, especially in television and film, for a casting director to put an actor forward for a part precisely because he so closely resembles the appearance and personality of the character in the script. If you think you've been cast for this reason, you'd be well advised to keep your character-work simple and just 'deliver the goods'. Once your employers know that you're reliable and can act truthfully, they may take a bit more of a risk with you next time.

So are there still opportunities for the actor who enjoys playing people different from himself, who wants to be what we might call a 'transformational character actor'? Thankfully, yes. Theatre can still offer real character-acting challenges, especially if you're cast to play more than one role in the same piece – something which is now fairly common due to shrinking theatre budgets. In a typical John Godber play you may be called on to play numerous roles including some stereotypes, all of which need to be markedly different. And there are other areas of employment for transformational character actors: the corporate video sector, radio plays, the live role-play sector within business – all require the actor to be something of a chameleon.

You will want, in rehearsal, to add something of your own to a role. The director will want to ensure that your choices make sense within the parameters of the play. To balance these two 'wants', you will need, above all, a clear eye and strong, versatile technique. But where to find that technique?

Some of the tips I offer in this book spring from the advice of Konstantin Stanislavski. Early in the last century Stanislavski mapped out a comprehensive system for actor training, and his work still forms the cornerstone for pretty well all modern actor training in the West. He teaches how to make a script more easily digestible by dividing it into units. He also teaches about circles of attention, about tempo-rhythm in the voice and tempo-rhythm in the body, about emotion memory, about all sorts of tricks and techniques and exercises. His system has, like that other best-seller the Bible, been quoted and misquoted and re-written and 'improved'; but it has certainly helped many actors find their way. Some, including David Mamet, think Stanislavski has created a baffling system which has harmed actors' ability to act well. Others (myself included) feel that although Stanislavski wrote much that is still of value to actors, some of his writings now seem remote. There was a thrilling period in the early days of naturalistic theatre, in the late 19th century, when actors and playwrights were at times ahead of those new scientists – the psychologists – in understanding human behaviour. But some of Stanislavski's general observations on human behaviour, and how to replicate it, are perhaps less relevant now, in the 21st century, than they were when written. And while much has been added by talented and well-meaning disciples, some of them really have further muddied the water.

Horses for courses, as the saying goes. If you're attracted to the task of understanding Stanislavski's vision of acting – or those of his disciples (or rivals) – and you're willing to work systematically through the various layers of those onions, then your rewards may be rich indeed. Be aware, though, that these are demanding disciplines, and as such they tend to require an intense intellectual commitment from the pupil. It can be healthy for actors, and for their teachers, to engage with philosophies and psychologies which seem heavyweight and important; the intensive study which they demand can at best lead to excellent discipline, and a confidence-boosting sense of elevated status. At worst, though, they can lead to a secret sense of inadequacy, buried under an overblown sense of elevated status.

I'm not at all sure, then, that actors need to be intellectuals. Thinkers, yes; researchers, of course; collectors, definitely. Over the years I've chatted with a number of creative people working at the very top of their discipline. In every case I've been struck by their humour, their love of their craft, and their commitment to its demystification. I love that. It's inclusive; it allows people to talk about things without feeling that they have to join a secret society or develop extra brain power.

So is this book for you? Well, not if you're looking for another secret society to join. But if you already have the actor's basic talent for looking and sounding spontaneous at the drop of a hat, and you'd like to become much more versatile – if you'd like to learn how to change with the ease of a chameleon – then read on. What this book is intended to deliver is a common-sense, jargon-free, step-by-step guide to helping you act characters truthfully.

The book is, therefore, mostly about communication – the things people do which others can see and hear. These things tell us what someone is thinking and feeling; they help us to understand the relationship between two people; they help us to recognise how someone feels about their surroundings. The signs a person gives out through their body and their voice afford us all the clues we need to understand them. So what are these signs?

We will consider all the key characteristics of behaviour – real, changeable, everyday human behaviour, both vocal and physical. You'll be guided through an understanding of the things you do in everyday life; you'll learn how, and why, you change your behaviour as a result of changing circumstances. With each behaviour 'type' you'll be offered a precise description of the behaviour, including behavioural opposites and examples from the animal world. You will learn subtler versions of the behaviour, and you'll see glimpses of how changes of behaviour are often used by writers and actors for comic or dramatic effect. Finally, you'll be given practical advice on how to use your new awareness of each behaviour when developing a character; and you will be guided through simple, practical exercises to help you sharpen your skill and awareness, and thus your versatility.

Will this book then turn you into a skilful transformational character actor? I hope so. At the very least I hope that through reading the book, and through exploring its ideas via the exercises, you'll become a more confident and sophisticated communicator. All actors engage in the task of actively creating stories for an audience. Whether the actor chooses to do so by using his own personality, or whether he prefers to melt away his own personality and create a new one to fit the story, is largely up to him and his director. It's certainly valid for an actor to seek out and develop, in the part he's been given, all the things which audiences need to know. And sometimes an actor will be asked to inhabit a world which is foreign to him. What's important is that the actor's choices towards the role he develops are honourable; that they do justice to the character.

To do justice to a character, though, you will need to do justice to the play. You will need to use good detective skills to work out what is going on, and to identify how your character dovetails with the rest of the characters in the play. You will need to plan.

section 1: **the skills for the job**

In this Section we will be considering the range and type of skills which an actor should possess in order to operate effectively. This 'skills inventory' offers you the chance to see how you measure up for the job of acting, and makes suggestions on where to seek further help if you need it.

What then are the qualities you would need, in order to function as an effective professional? Before the first line is spoken in the rehearsal room, before you've even thought about character – before, indeed, the first CV and photo are to be posted – what should a professional actor be capable of doing?

For me, there are nine such essential skills:

- knowing how to achieve a state of full physical and mental relaxation

- being able to work creatively with stamina, determination, and a sense of fun

- understanding how to apply intelligent analysis to a text or situation

- being able to demonstrate non-verbal behaviour between people

- knowing how to use your voice effectively in public

- being able to create and maintain a sense of reality in imagined circumstances

- being able to adapt performance style and size to suit the medium

- knowing how to manage and act on criticism

- being willing to actively network with people in the industry

Let's now look at each of these skills in turn.

Knowing how to achieve a state of full physical and mental relaxation

An overarching skill which you will need as an actor – the ability to relax physically and mentally under pressure. Relaxation is important for a number of reasons. Firstly, and most obviously, you will need to be able to feel confident under stressful circumstances (of which there are many – starting with auditions). Secondly, the ability to selectively relax muscles will help you to overcome tension-related barriers to effective performance, such as tension in the throat (which harms the voice). Thirdly – this sounds a bit arty, but stay with it – the state of being fully physically and mentally relaxed can be used as an effective meditative state from which to build a mental and physical profile that is appropriate to the character you're playing. Put simply, you can stop being too locked into being 'you', make yourself a sort of blank canvas, and create your character from there.

Fortunately, physical relaxation is a skill which is relatively easy to develop with practice. But you will need a good teacher, or at the very least a partner who can help you spot the difference between 'relaxed' and 'slightly tensed'. Ideally you will be a student, or a prospective student, on a reputable training course for performers. If you're not currently training there's a good chance that some kind of initial relaxation training is available near you: all cities, and most towns, have appropriate evening or day classes in physical relaxation, although it's likely to come under a more impressive banner such as yoga or stress management. Do your research: the key to effective physical relaxation is to work regularly on isolating, tensing and relaxing the various muscles of the body, until you can do so at will. This takes practice.

If you can't make it to a good weekly class, or if you do your research and can't find one, you could try teaching yourself to relax using one of the relaxation CDs available on the market. Indeed I would advise that you use both class and CD, as you need to spend time teaching yourself to relax, and that's not always easy in a room full of other students. The best CDs are positive in tone, and are carefully paced to allow you to imagine that the teacher is actually there with you.

Some relaxation CDs are more to do with therapy than with relaxation: if you can, 'audition' them first (try the local public library). What you need is a calm, controlled, step-by-step recording of how to take yourself through staged relaxation, spoken by someone whose voice you feel able to trust. There are some words in the Appendix ('Relaxation Exercise with Visualisation') which you might like to learn and use; you could even record the words yourself and play them back as you relax. Practise every day: it will definitely help you in your daily life.

So much for physical relaxation, but what about mental stress? The mental challenges of being an actor are well-documented – from the pressure to recall lines in public, to the confidence-sapping experience of being judged and often rejected on the basis of simply how you look. What can you do to cope with such pressure? One solution, which has come to actors partly via sports psychology, is to use visualisation – meaning a controlled use of the imagination to build a sense of confidence and self-belief. A golfer will imagine sweetly putting the ball from the edge of the green; the actor can imagine in detail any number of positive outcomes, from playing a forthcoming scene with skill and truth, to hearing his agent phone to say 'you've got the part'. Since actors rely on energetic use of the imagination as a central tool in their job, it should come easier for them than for most. But, again, active imagining needs practice.

Being able to work creatively with stamina, determination, and a sense of fun

Actors are hardly unique in requiring these qualities in the work environment. But acting is a job which is full of contradictions, and these carry their own pressures. You will need stamina to cope with the long hours in the rehearsal room or on set; much of your time will be spent in idle suspension as you wait your turn to rehearse or record (I waited three days to shoot anything on my first film). And when the call comes you must be totally ready for action.

There are plenty of banana skins to slip on, even if you're being treated well: last-minute script or schedule changes, technical hitches, a sudden loss of confidence or health, fellow actors who annoyingly save their 'real' performance for the camera or the stage. So you have to stay focused on the job, listen to the people who need you to listen, and be determined to acquit yourself well. You can do some obvious things to help yourself: keep healthy; try to sleep well; and work on your ability to keep energy in reserve by using mental and physical relaxation techniques. Many actors have a relaxing solo hobby which they carry around with them such as reading, sketching, writing, doing crosswords. Learn to tick over: if you rev up too much you'll eventually run out of fuel. But you can't afford to switch your engine off completely; leave the engine on and put yourself in neutral.

Determination is an essential quality for any actor. Modern acting is not really pure art, I'm afraid; when you boil it all down it's first and foremost a commercial service. You do a job for an agreed fee during specified hours. If the artistic muse doesn't arrive – well you'll just have to act anyway. And then at the next audition you're either right for the part or you're not: if not, you will still be unemployed. After a run of knock-backs at auditions you'll feel like giving up.

Don't. Be determined, be patient, and hunt out the next audition. It's occasionally overlooked during an actor's training that he is a *business*. You offer your appearance and your ability to act to schedule; and you do so in an overcrowded market. If you don't have an agent, you must find your own work. If you do have an agent, some of the time you will still have to find your own work. You need to be determined.

This all sounds very serious, and of course it is. So where's the fun in being an actor? It's there, and you need to find it and embrace it. You can help yourself maintain a positive creative working attitude whether in or out of work by remaining 'playful'. A professional actor is paid to act because people consider that he is really good at sharing the things in his imagination. However serious and committed you become as an actor, you will always be imagining, playing. That's why, at heart, acting is tremendous fun. It must be – it's a passionate hobby for millions of amateurs worldwide. So don't take yourself too seriously. And don't hold up a shoot or a rehearsal to make a serious point, unless you're certain that the director will want to hear it. Keep a sense of perspective, and keep a sense of fun.

Understanding how to apply intelligent analysis to a text or situation

Again, there are no unique skills required for an actor to assess and understand a text or situation, and a good director will have strategies in hand to help his actors learn important things about the context of a play. The planning stage is crucial; Section Two explores one method for preparing for rehearsal and performance.

At the start of the rehearsal stage in theatre there may well be some brief discussion on matters such as the playwright's intention, the personal histories of key characters, the presence of subtext. Such discussions can be very helpful in guiding the actor towards creating the 'world' of the play in his own imagination. But time is precious in 'the business', and, as rehearsal periods shrink further and further, so must all discussion be seen to serve the task of communicating the play to the audience. These days it's mostly up to the actor to analyse his script and research the world around the play. The more remote the piece is from the actor's own world, the more important it is to conduct high-quality research, and to come to some agreement with director and other actors regarding the world these characters inhabit. Everything from politics, culture, food, history, social and sexual mores, religion, economic circumstances, climate, class structure, and time of year is fair game for the actor's microscope.

Being able to demonstrate non-verbal behaviour between people

An understanding of, and ability to demonstrate, physical behaviour will be central to your task of communicating effectively to an audience. Accordingly, a complete Section is dedicated to the development of these practical skills.

Knowing how to use the voice effectively in public

Public speaking topped spiders and even *death* in a recent survey of people's greatest phobias. Yet public speaking is central to virtually any acting performance. So how do actors cope? Once again, relaxation technique is important, along with a focused, positive state of mind. There are some excellent and highly specialised practical handbooks available, which can help the actor become confident and competent in the effective development of vocal technique (see Further Reading in the Appendix). Practice in rehearsal and performance is obviously essential.

High-quality technical vocal training will leave you feeling confident in voice use onstage and on set; the best way to develop this is undoubtedly to work with a good voice coach, backing this up with a good book or two. Once this confidence and competence is in place you'll feel able to use and vary such characteristics as tone, inflection, note, loudness, pace, accent and diction. We will explore these aspects of voice and speech, along with some basics on voice use, in two full Sections.

Being able to create and maintain a sense of reality in imagined circumstances

Actors basically pretend. They pretend to be other people in circumstances imagined by a writer. If the actor concentrates really hard on the pretence, and if the writing is good, the audience will probably be drawn in and invest belief in the situations portrayed on the stage, and the story can be told.

But what can you do to pretend so convincingly that you really start to believe? A smart actor will use everything around him onstage to 'trick' himself into believing that he is a character in a real situation, rather than just an actor in a show. Set, costume, mood created through lighting, and props are all visual stimuli which can help an actor to believe in the situation onstage. Sound, too, can be a valuable stimulus to belief.

A lot of what you're required to do as an actor is crazy when you think about it. As a professional actor I've been, variously: a spaceman who has his heart torn out by an alien; a businessman who is zapped onto the hard drive of a computer; a psychotic armed robber who terrorises pubgoers; and a litter-bug comedy cop who is chased down a street by a gang of schoolchildren. At drama school my teachers didn't do a 'how to react to having your heart ripped from your chest' workshop; but they did help me rediscover the sheer pleasure of playing games. An actor is paid to take risks, to take characters into those exciting areas that normal people tend to avoid at all costs. The call of duty might require you to strip naked, be really ugly, kiss strangers (of both genders), stand screaming on top of a mountain, weep in a crowded room – perhaps even all at once. Such madness needs practice, unless you're mad already. So practise actively imagining things. And practise remembering things from your past. Practise re-experiencing things, so that you're not afraid of calling on memories and sensations from your own life. Exercise your imagination as if it were a muscle, because like a muscle it'll strengthen with repeated use. And improvise – practise the exhilarating craft of making things up without a script. Get together with a few acting students who are trusted friends, meet somewhere safe, and dare to have fun. And read on: the final Section of this book, entitled 'Inner Life', explores in more detail how to harness your imagination.

Spontaneity in performance is obviously central to being believed. Some people can create a sense of spontaneity at will; others can't. And those who can't will never be convincing actors. Maintaining spontaneity with repetition is not easy, yet this is what television and film routinely demand. Staying spontaneous during a three-show theatre run is not too difficult, because the adrenaline rush keeps you sharp. But what happens when the nerves wear off, or when the pattern of an actor's performance – his stage movement, his vocal inflection, his pacing and so on – becomes fixed through repetition? An actor who has been performing the same role for several weeks, or even months, must find ways to keep his performance fresh each time. Again, we will be looking at ways to retain spontaneity later in the book.

Being able to adapt performance style and size to suit the medium

One of the more difficult skills which you'll need to develop is the ability to turn up or bring down the level of your performance in response to the needs of the venue or medium. In any theatre, your intended communication must reach the entire audience. In all but the tiniest of studio theatres it becomes necessary for you to project your performance in order to be understood. And a different sort of awareness is needed for acting in the round, compared to other types of staging. Voice projection is obviously an important skill to develop, but what about use of the body? Technically, a small gesture which is stimulated by a particular emotional response may need to be enlarged – without losing the 'truth' behind the action. Also, your physical performance will need to be subtly controlled, so that gestures are limited to those which carry intended meaning.

In a medium such as film, all intended communication must again reach the entire audience; however, there are very different demands on you. Believability is vital; you must be seen to be 'thinking the thoughts', as audiences look to your eyes and face for meaning. And since your face may be 20 feet high on a cinema screen, you'd better be convincing.

The challenge at the heart of this skill is to marry the instinctive with the technical. It's no good being emotionally truthful if your audience can't hear you; and it's not much fun if you can hear an actor clearly but there's little truth in what he is saying and doing. What is needed is good technique – the ability to blend psychologically and emotionally truthful acting with excellent audience communication.

In my experience, actors instinctively lean towards one of three 'types'. I call these the Inhabiter, the Storyteller, and the Classicist. I think it's useful to know which type of actor you most closely represent; it can give you confidence in your strengths, and can help you to identify your areas of weakness. If you're not sure which is most 'you', you might start by asking your fellow actors.

- The **Inhabiter** needs to 'become' a character. This type of actor applies immense focus to the task of engaging psychologically and emotionally with the circumstances within a character's story. If you're acting onstage or on set with an Inhabiter, it feels very personal. At best, he is deeply moving for an audience to observe; at worst, he can be resentful of an audience's presence, and this can hamper his willingness to reach them with good technique. An Inhabiter needs to remember his audience, empathise with them, and help them out with good vocal and physical communication.

- The **Storyteller** loves to tell the story of the play to the audience. In his performance, communication is focused primarily on this task, and even if he never actually looks at the audience, he's always aware of them, reaching through the divide to share his character's experience with them. Act with a Storyteller and you'll always feel reminded of the presence of an audience. From the audience's perspective the Storyteller can be an exhilarating and hugely entertaining performer; at worst, he can lack engagement with his fellow actors, and can lack truth.

- The **Classicist** is drawn to text which is filled with imagery and is challenging to deliver. He has – most likely through earlier education – developed a sense of comfort with the textual style of 'the classics', be they Shakespeare, Wilde or even Berkoff in neo-classical mode. At best, he combines the skills of the other two 'types' to tell a character's story truthfully, while 'hand-holding' his audience. At worst, he can overindulge in the poetic nature of the text, charming us with his speaking while obscuring the story with his showboating style. His skill combines the best of the other two, but adds a sense of fearlessness towards 'difficult' text.

So which type of acting is best? In truth, no one type is 'better' than the others; but if you become aware of the challenges and the pitfalls which accompany each type, you'll be better placed to make good acting choices as you prepare for performance.

Knowing how to manage and act on criticism

Throughout their working lives, actors receive criticism which is often pretty direct and personal. And it can hurt. It is after all undeniably you who is being criticised: your talent, your looks, your voice, your age, your range, your intellect, even your sense of confidence. Even a playwright can rationalise criticism of their work by thinking of it as a play, a script, something they created which is now over there on that stage. For the actor, the finger points straight at him: the thing being criticised is the same thing that goes home after the show and climbs into bed. So actors may as well get used to it coming their way, and try to manage it. Managing it means interpreting it, and doing something useful with it. (My first national newspaper review labelled my West End debut as 'charismatic'. My then agent read it and said, 'We don't see it, Paul.' I use the first bit of criticism as a confidence boost, and I chuckle about the second. What else can I do?)

After an audition, a professional actor might reasonably expect some useful and honest feedback. They don't get it. Ever! (Well, almost never.) A much better source for useful critical feedback is a workshop, such as those run for actors at National Actors Centres (see www.actorscentre.co.uk). You'll often find yourself working with an experienced professional who, because he is being paid simply to run a workshop, will answer your questions honestly. You'll gain practice at your craft, and you might even make a useful contact. Which leads on to:

Being willing to actively network with people in the industry

There isn't space in a book on acting skills to explore this quality in any detail, but it is an absolutely crucial one nonetheless. Any business which offers a new product to the market will sensibly focus a lot of time and energy on promotion and advertising. An actor is no different, except that the potential buyer of an actor's services is already awash with alternatives which are tried, tested and trusted, and they don't like you cold-calling one bit!

There is good advice out there for any actor who wants to reach potential employers (see Further Reading), and of course for a trained actor the process typically starts with a professional-quality self-introduction via a posted CV and photo. If you're going to launch yourself as a professional actor but you don't have an agent to make the introductions for you – bad luck. You'll have to get writing anyway. If you do land an agent – well, good – but don't expect them to get you too much in the way of auditions, though a good agent will also be able to fix up informal (and hugely valuable) chats with casting directors. Some actors offer showreels on video or on DVD, others have their own websites. All British actors are in Spotlight, the casting directory. In acting, visibility is all: you've got to try to be at the top of the pile of photos and not in the bottom drawer, or in the bin. You'll need to be capable of a long-running campaign of friendly harassment by post. (I once turned up for an audition at Granada TV and was handed a package by a highly amused assistant in the casting office. 'We thought you might be able to use these,' she grinned, handing me 20 or so identical photos of myself.)

A professional actor will normally meet casting directors and directors on their 'home turf', and in such situations he is steered through the process on their terms, which can leave little opportunity to make a lasting impression. A brave actor will seek out the moments where directors, casting directors and agents come out of their bunkers and face the great unwashed of the acting profession present and future – the workshops, the visits to see a show, the talks to students. If you do launch yourself as an actor, and you find yourself next to them in the bar, say hello. Be genuine, friendly, but not overbearing. And shock them by asking them about themselves. Shock them even more by listening, and there's a chance that they'll remember you!

section 2: **planning to act**

This Section looks at the planning stage of acting. Actors need to plan for acting so that they can set to work rehearsing with confidence, knowing that they understand the story of the play, the likely personality of their own character, and the nature of key relationships within the play.

To enable you to plan effectively, this Section will take you through how to use three key planning Tools. Tool Number 1 is the Character Profile Sheet. This is a 'collecting point' for all the research you carry out when you are reading and re-reading the play prior to, and during, rehearsal. You'll be shown how each category listed on the Character Profile Sheet contributes to your understanding of your character, of the play, and of key relationships. You'll see how Setting the Status (Tool Number 2) enables you to further explore relationships with insight and confidence; and you'll learn how Power Matters (Tool Number 3) in understanding why key characters allow others to behave the way they do.

At the end of our analysis of each of the Tools, you will, within the next four Sections of the book, be offered Acting Tips, along with Solo Exercises and Partnered Exercises. Where appropriate we will also refer to published playscripts, and to one script in particular – Anton Chekhov's fascinatingly restrained *Three Sisters*. In the Appendix you'll find a completed Character Profile Sheet for the character of Natasha from *Three Sisters*. As this book progresses we will refer to Natasha, and to scenes involving Natasha (in the chronological order in which they occur), to consider how various Tools might be used in performance.

Tool No. 1: The Character Profile Sheet

What do you usually do before you get to work on learning lines and rehearsing? What does a director expect from you, the moment you arrive at the first rehearsal? Picture the scene: you hold the script in your hand for the first time and – what? Count your lines? Colour them in with a highlighter pen? Read your lines aloud to 'hear' your character speak for the first time? Start learning the lines straight off? All very tempting (and I'll admit to having done all of the above at some point). But if you want to create a real, believable, three-dimensional character *who belongs in the same script and story as the other characters*, you'll need to do some planning first.

At the back of this book in the Appendix you'll find a **blank Character Profile Sheet**. This is a single-page document, a copy of which you should begin to complete in pencil when you start work on creating a new character. The idea is that, before rehearsals begin, you have a single place to pull together the discoveries you make as you read and re-read the script.

As rehearsals begin, each actor's sheet can be altered and added to as new discoveries take place. The sheet also acts as a focus for discussion, so that two actors can discuss, say, conflicts between their characters by referring to their own research. It seems to work as a good way of keeping actors in the same play!

Each of the areas which we will explore in this Section has a matching area on the Character Profile Sheet. When you've worked through this Section, have a go at completing a Character Profile Sheet on yourself – the character of You. It's quite sobering to stand back after completing such a sheet to reflect on how you came to be who you are, as a result of the some of the things explored below.

In the Appendix you'll find **Guidelines on how to complete the Character Profile Sheet**. There's also a completed Character Profile Sheet, which is offered simply as an example of how the completed version might look.

Unearthing the clues: start with the facts

So, after the first reading of the play, what do you already know about your character? Some playwrights are more generous than others in supplying background information on your character's life; some prefer to be vague; but many facts are obvious anyway. Roughly how old is the character? What family do you know of? What's the character's occupation, and what did they do before that? Where do they live? What events have taken place in their life before the play begins? These are pure facts, and these facts help to give you a clear starting point from which to get to know the character. Add them to your Character Profile Sheet in the **Facts** section. Don't be tempted to ignore any of these facts – the playwright has put them there for a reason, and if you want your character to remain in the same story as the other characters, these facts should not be ignored. Once you start comparing your character's facts with the facts about other characters, you should start to see how the jigsaw has been put together.

Example: Natasha from *Three Sisters*

From the playscript we can deduce the following about Natasha:

- she is a local girl
- during the story she is engaged to, then marries, Andrei
- she marries above her social class
- she gains wealth through marriage
- she 'runs' the house once she is married
- she becomes mother to Sophie and Bobik
- her husband is a gambler and a would-be academic
- she learns to speak French

- she believes that servants should be sacked when they are too old to work well
- she begins an affair with Protopopov

History matters

" ... other people, friends, family, sociologists, the media, they're the ones who tell us who we are. I mean, let's face it, if tomorrow you or I lost everyone around us, we'd instantly become sort of non-people, wouldn't we? "

Alex in Virtual Reality *by Alan Ayckbourn*

A person's sense of identity is strongly influenced by other people. It seems a fair bet that if you've spent the best part of your life being told you're stupid by everyone around you, then you're unlikely to pursue a career in astrophysics. On the other hand, if others have convinced you over time that you're really quite a witty person, then chances are you'll wear this label like a sheriff's badge and be as witty as you can at every turn. Nicknames are labels too – and labels which describe an attitude or behaviour are particularly hard to shake off. 'Lazy bones', 'moan-a-lot', 'Lord Snooty' – imagine how it might affect you to be called such names day in, day out.

Successes and failures in life cast long shadows. If you did badly in important school exams, then in later life you will probably still wear a label which says 'No Good at Exams' – whatever the cause. By the time you reach adulthood you will have countless labels from parents, peers, pedagogues and partners – so many that it would be hard indeed to sum up who 'you' are in a single phrase. Of course, the only labels that really affect your sense of self are the ones of which you're aware. If the polite next-door neighbour secretly thinks you're a boring and self-obsessed acting student, but they never actually tell you, then you may go on 'fascinating' them with theatrical anecdotes for years to come.

What's true for people in life is also true for characters in plays. A good playwright or scriptwriter may well weave in labels which are there to be unpicked. As a committed transformational character actor, you should rise to the challenge: winkle them out, line them up, and decide how much they matter to the characters. When you've done this, add them to the '**What you have heard others say about you**' section of the Character Profile Sheet. Now you can start to look with more confidence through the eyes of your character. A word of warning, though. A famous actor did something like this once when working on a play. After collecting a sizeable bunch of quotes from other characters, he mentioned his research to his director, who frowned, then observed, 'Well, of course, they could all be lying.'

Example: Natasha from *Three Sisters*

People say the following things in front of Natasha:

- 'I love you – I want you to be my wife' (Andrei)
- 'you're so young, so beautiful, so wonderful!' (Andrei)
- 'you were so rude to Nanny just now' (Olga)
- 'the way she's going around you'd think it was her who started the fire' (Masha)

Things that Natasha may have overheard:

- 'It isn't Bobik that's sick, it's her up there ... stupid woman!' (Masha)
- 'The way she dresses! – it's absolutely pitiful! And her cheeks shining, absolutely scrubbed!' (Masha)

A question of personality

How would you describe your character's personality? For that matter, how would you describe your *own* personality? Like you, a well-written character will be full of patterns and contradictions. Some actors are very shy. Apparently calm people can suddenly become aggressive. 'Born' leaders can lose confidence in themselves. This is true in life – as in drama. Totally predictable people are the least interesting people; totally predictable characters in plays are the least interesting characters.

Imagine you're cast as a vicar in a play. How would you describe the personality of the vicar? The stereotypical vicar in modern drama will always be well-meaning, helpful, easily embarrassed, possibly a slight stutterer. That's what the audience is expecting when you walk onstage, or enter onscreen, wearing your dog-collar. So far so predictable; and in a comedy built around stereotypes, this may well be just what the writer intends (and what the audience wants). But what if it's not a comedy of stereotypes? What if the playwright intends a character who is more 'real'?

The temptation is often to 'do the opposite' – even if it's not really in the play. Give the vicar a crisis of faith; make him (or her) rude, unhelpful – perhaps alcoholic? Anything, in fact, to make them interesting. But resist. Trust the playwright. Look for new clues to the character's real personality. And remember that a person's job doesn't necessarily define them; my village's local vicar – a former policeman – is now a hugely successful children's author.

Read the script afresh and run a personality assessment of your character. I use part of a personality test which has been employed in the 'real world', one which was created by the late Professor Hans Eysenck (see Further Reading). It allows you to identify the full range of behaviours and attitudes shown by your character throughout the play; and it lets you see what your character's predominant personality tends to be, so that you might conclude that your character is a stable introvert, or perhaps a neurotic extrovert. It works as a way of 'seeing' the whole personality. The test is below the title word '**Personality**' on the blank Character Profile Sheet in the Appendix.

Example: Natasha from *Three Sisters*

For the three sisters and the servants, Natasha is something of an outsider, coming, as she does, from a lower social class and from the local area. She marries a man who gambles and is unhappy in his career, and she takes on an unfamiliar role as effective head of the running of the house. We see her fretting about her children, and we glean that she eventually starts an affair. Under these circumstances her behaviour in the scenes within the play reveals much edginess and insecurity.

Looking at the left-hand side of the 'Personality' section on the Character Profile Sheet, there seems little evidence of unstable behaviour, other that she can at times be talkative. In contrast, most of the categories on the right-hand side seem to apply: she is by turns impulsive and aggressive (e.g. when turning on the servant Anfisa for daring to sit down in her presence); rigid (e.g. insisting on taking Irina's room from her); anxious (e.g. over her children's health); unsociable (e.g. cancelling the entertainers). As an actor preparing to play Natasha, you have reason to think of her as quite a neurotic person: perhaps a little more extrovert than introvert, but neurotic nonetheless. Such an analysis of a character's personality can be a warning to you. If you play her simply as a neurotic 'type', you run the risk of being predictable. So look too for the warmth and stability in her, even if it is only somewhere in the background.

Tool No. 2: Setting the Status
It's fun to play on the seesaw – usually

> Walk into a dressing room and say 'I got the part' and everyone will congratulate you, but will feel lowered. Say 'They said I was too old' and people commiserate, but cheer up perceptibly.
>
> *Keith Johnstone, writing in* Impro

Keith Johnstone writes of the 'seesaw principle', whereby a person's sense of status (I think of it as their sense of importance, in relation to others) is strongly affected by the physical behaviour of someone else. I go down, you go up; you go down, I go up. Johnstone is brilliant at exposing how we all, consciously and sub-consciously, play status games all the time. He offers valuable lessons for the actor in how to develop better status-playing skills.

There are three distinct, but related, types of status, which we all use. The first is the type over which we have least control: social status.

Social status
Social status attaches to you as a result of how society views people in your position. There is a pecking order in society which dictates that a queen is more important than a tramp, that a bank manager has higher social status than an office cleaner. It's important to be aware of social status before you play around with the other two types, as your 'normal' social status is always lurking there in the background when people interact with you. Next time you're in a room full of strangers, imagine that one of them is a rich and successful rock musician who is hoping to avoid being spotted: you can almost see the glow around them as they begin to stand out from ordinary mortals.

Social status has much to do with power. The more power you have to influence others, the higher up the social hierarchy you'll go. Rock stars have incredible power when they are successful, but once they stop selling records they are on a steep and slippery slope.

It's useful to know about social status because conflict in plays often comes from a character losing, or gaining, social status. King Lear's steady loss of social status is at the heart of his tragedy. Bottom's hike in social status among the fairy people, despite his having sprouted the head of an ass, is at the heart of the comedy. Films make the switch often; the hit Eddie Murphy/Dan Ackroyd comedy *Trading Places* is perhaps one of the best-known.

Play study: The Admirable Crichton *by J M Barrie*
J M Barrie's inspired play *The Admirable Crichton*, written in the early 20th century, takes the comedy and the drama of social-

status 'switching' to its highest level. His play maroons an upper-class English family on a desert island, and places them at the mercy of their ever-resourceful butler.

Act One sees Ernest preparing an amusement which involves summoning the servants 'upstairs' for tea with his aristocratic friends. Before long, the party is in full and unbearably awkward swing, with Crichton's fellow (subordinate) servants being forced to attempt polite conversation with Ernest's upper-class friends. The emerging nub of Barrie's play is raised in conversation between Crichton and Lord Loam:

LORD LOAM
Can't you see, Crichton, that our divisions into classes are artificial, that if we were to return to nature, which is the aspiration of my life, all would be equal?

CRICHTON
If I may make so bold as to contradict your lordship –

LORD LOAM *(with an effort)*
Go on.

CRICHTON
The divisions into classes, my lord, are not artificial. They are the natural outcome of a civilised society. *(To LADY MARY)* There must always be a master and servants in all civilised communities, my lady, for it is natural, and whatever is natural is right.

Act Two begins following the shipwreck, as the truth of Crichton's belief is put to the test. Ernest, selected friends and servants struggle to adapt to desert-island living. Crichton's resourcefulness and energy quickly bring him status and authority as he sets about building a home for the party; Ernest sits uselessly on an upturned bucket and composes verse. But not for long:

CRICHTON *(to LADY MARY)*
> ... until a ship comes we are three men who are going to do our best for you ladies.

LADY MARY *(with a curl of the lip)*
> Mr. Ernest does no work.

CRICHTON *(cheerily)*
> But he will, my lady.

LADY MARY
> I doubt it.

CRICHTON *(confidently, but perhaps thoughtlessly)*
> No work – no dinner – will make a great change in Mr. Ernest.

LADY MARY
> No work – no dinner. When did you invent that rule, Crichton?

CRICHTON *(loaded with bamboo)*
> I didn't invent it, my lady. I seem to see it growing all over the island ...

Act Three – entitled 'The Happy Home' – brings us up to date with events of the previous two years, which have seen Crichton emerge as the unchallenged leader of the group, a man who has built a home bursting with desert-island luxuries. We learn that, indeed, everyone is changed; Lady Mary has become a huntress, and even Ernest now pulls his weight, albeit under threat of 'the bucket', a water punishment which his former butler imposes when deemed necessary. Crichton, now known to all as 'The Gov.', turns his full force on the adoring Lady Mary:

CRICHTON

I am lord over all. They are but hewers of wood and drawers of water for me. These shores are mine. Why should I hesitate; I have no longer any doubt. I do believe I am doing the right thing. Dear Polly, I have grown to love you; are you afraid to mate with me? *(She rocks her arms; no words will come from her.)* 'I was a king in Babylon, And you were a Christian slave.'

LADY MARY *(bewitched)*

You are the most wonderful man I have ever known, and I am not afraid …

But as they all dance to celebrate the forthcoming union between 'The Gov.' and Lady Mary, a shot signals the arrival of a rescue party of English sailors.

Within moments, the 'natural' order of things starts to melt back to the old ways.

Act Four return us to 'the other island' – England. Ernest has penned a shockingly untruthful revision of events on the desert island, in which he positions himself as hero and provider – a version which is supported heartily by his aristocratic fellow-adventurers. In this version Crichton plays only a small supporting role as the reliable butler. Yet Crichton seems happy to play along with the deception. The play ends with this private exchange between Crichton and Lady Mary:

LADY MARY

Do you despise me, Crichton? *(The man who could never tell a lie makes no answer.)* You are the best man among us.

CRICHTON

On an island, my lady, perhaps; but in England, no.

LADY MARY

Then there's something wrong with England.

CRICHTON

My lady, not even from you can I listen to a word against England.

LADY MARY

Tell me one thing: you have not lost your courage?

CRICHTON

No, my lady.

(She goes. He turns out the lights.)

So ends one of the greatest social-status 'switch' comedies of all time – with a warning, perhaps, to the audience of the time to look to their own conscience.

A feature of social-status switching is, of course, that characters react to changing circumstances by altering what they say, and what they do. What they say, we can call their verbal status; what they do, their physical status.

Verbal status

Every spoken word or phrase carries with it a verbal status. The speaker's words, and the attitude behind those words, automatically claim a position for the speaker on the status seesaw. If the two people on the seesaw have opposite social status – a queen and a tramp, for example – then the stage is set for verbal status activity which undermines the established relative social status. The most obvious way to use verbal status to claim top spot on the seesaw is to insult someone horribly, and sound as if you really mean it. The more unpleasant the image you can create in people's minds, the lower you're forcing the person being insulted. Helena and Hermia's furious barrage of insults aimed at one another's height in Shakespeare's *A Midsummer Night's*

Dream, stands as a good example. I've marked the verbal status insults in bold; as you'll see, the seesaw hammers up and down as speedily as the audience can follow it:

HELENA

... What, will you tear impatient answers from my gentle tongue?
Fie, fie, you **counterfeit**, you **puppet** you!

HERMIA

Puppet? Why so? Ay that way goes the game.
Now I perceive that she hath made compare
Between our statures. She hath urged her height,
And with her personage – her tall personage –
Her height, forsooth – she hath prevailed with him.
– And are you grown so high in his esteem
Because **I am so dwarfish** and so **low**?
How low am I thou **painted maypole**? Speak
How low am I? I am not yet so low
But that my nails can reach unto thine eyes.

HELENA

I pray you though you mock me gentlemen,
Let her not hurt me. I was never curst,
I have no gift at all in shrewishness –
I am a right maid for my cowardice.
Let her not strike me. You perhaps may think
Because **she is something lower than myself**
That I can match her ...

Followed a few lines later with –

HELENA

O when she's angry **she is keen and shrewd**.
She was a vixen when she went to school
And **though she is but little she is fierce**.

HERMIA

Little again! Nothing but low and little!
Why will you suffer her to flout me thus?
Let me come to her ...

At which point Lysander joins in with –

LYSANDER

Get you gone you **dwarf**!
You **minimus of hind'ring knot-grass made**!
You **bead**! you **acorn**!

A Midsummer Night's Dream, Act 3 Scene 2

It follows that the easiest way to offer someone else top spot on the seesaw is to compliment them, and to do it as sincerely as you can. The Duke of Gloucester (later King Richard the Third) plays this trick to the hilt in his seduction of Lady Anne, whose husband he has just killed. She's just spat at him for claiming he would be a better husband to her than her beloved Edward:

GLOUCESTER

Why dost thou spit at me?

ANNE

Would it were mortal poison, for thy sake!

GLOUCESTER

Never came poison from so sweet a place.

ANNE

Never hung poison on a fouler toad.
Out of my sight! Thou dost infect my eyes.

GLOUCESTER

Thine eyes, sweet lady, have infected mine.

ANNE

Would they were basilisks, to strike thee dead!

GLOUCESTER

I would they were, that I might die at once;
For now they kill me with a living death ...

King Richard The Third, Act 1 Scene 2

Add a believable criticism of yourself, so lowering your own status, and you confirm your partner's unassailable place as top dog. Some 16 lines later Anne hears this from the future King:

GLOUCESTER

I never sued to friend nor enemy;
My tongue could never learn sweet smoothing words;
But, now thy beauty is proposed my fee,
My proud heart sues and prompts my tongue to speak.

They marry shortly afterwards! Of course it's not usually straight-forward. In our modern society, extreme insults and unfettered compliments are regarded with distaste in almost equal measure. Insults, if sincere, are so status-lowering that they can lead to physical violence (think of football hooligans); extreme compliments lead straight to suspicion as to the speaker's motives. We humans are generally rather more sophisticated than that, so we use tricks and techniques to position ourselves on each seesaw we sit on, with each new partner.

Followers of a theory named Transactional Analysis define all our verbal status behaviour as falling into one of three types: adult, parent, or child. Whenever we speak, it's said, we uncon-sciously select one of these roles to make our point. And we often choose a role which is contrary to our social status. Reality TV shows love this theme: the 'bad' mother who rules her children by throwing tantrums; celebrities who behave like spoilt teenagers after downing a few drinks. But the social status 'switch' can also be intentional. The primary school teacher who asks a small child to help him solve a maths problem is using child-to-parent behaviour: the teacher secretly knows the answer, but raises the child's place on the seesaw, in order to give the child the confidence to have a go at the problem. Of course you'd have to hear the conversation to be sure: a sarcastic tone from the teacher, for example, would plunge the child back down by implying that he was not worthy of real respect. The insult in such a case is hidden in the tone of the voice, rather than in the actual words.

Transactional Analysis is a useful 'way in' to understanding verbal status. For a masterclass in the use of adult/parent/child verbal status, we can turn to Alan Ayckbourn's poignant and brilliantly observed *Mother Figure*. In this play – one of the 'Confusions' series of five interlinked plays – a bullying husband is brought to a standstill by the controlling parent-to-child behaviour of his neighbour, a desperately isolated young mother.

Play study: Mother Figure *by Alan Ayckbourn*

This one-act play takes place in the sitting room of LUCY, a stressed and permanently dressing-gowned married mother of small children. Neighbour ROSEMARY imposes herself to deliver a phone message from Lucy's absentee husband. But Lucy has descended so far into a world dominated by the needs of small children that she seems unable to manage 'proper' adult-to-adult interaction:

LUCY

Would you like a drink or something?

ROSEMARY

A drink? Oh – well – what's the time? Well – I don't know if I should. Half past – oh yes, well – why not? Yes, please. Why not? A little one.

LUCY

Orange or lemon?

ROSEMARY

I beg your pardon?

LUCY

Orange juice or lemon juice? Or you can have milk.

ROSEMARY

Oh, I see. I thought you meant ...

LUCY

Come on. Orange or lemon? I'm waiting ...

ROSEMARY

Is there a possibility of some coffee?

LUCY

No.

ROSEMARY

Oh.

LUCY

It'll keep you awake. I'll get you an orange, it's better for you.

ROSEMARY

Oh.

LUCY *(as she goes)*

Sit still. Don't run around. I won't be a minute.

So begins a wonderfully relentless sequence in which Lucy stays locked into parent-to-child mode of verbal status behaviour. Even the arrival of TERRY, Rosemary's controlling husband, fails to snap Lucy out of it. Terry draws his wife into an awkward argument about the role of men and women in the home, and they are both told off by Lucy, who then goes to fetch a drink for Terry (a glass of milk). While Lucy is out of the room Terry too slips into parent-child mode – aggressively this time – as he has 'words' with his wife:

TERRY

... we'll have less of that, too, if you don't mind.

ROSEMARY

What?

TERRY

All this business about me never going out of the house.

ROSEMARY

It's true.

TERRY

And even if it is true, you have no business saying it in front of other people.

ROSEMARY

Oh, honestly, Terry, you're so touchy. I can't say a thing right these days can I?

TERRY

Very little. Now you come to mention it.

The conversation takes a downward turn as, nursing her glass of orange juice, Rosemary launches an attack on a biscuit-munching Terry which pulls them both into child-to-child mode:

ROSEMARY

Niggle, niggle, niggle. You keep on at me the whole time. I'm frightened to open my mouth these days. I don't know what's got into you lately. You're in a filthy mood from the moment you get up till you go to bed ...

TERRY

What are you talking about?

ROSEMARY

Grumbling and moaning ...

TERRY

Oh, shut up.

ROSEMARY

You're a misery to live with these days, you really are.

TERRY

I said, shut up.

Terry snatches his wife's juice and finishes it – reducing her to tears. Lucy strides in and tells Terry off: he, in a sulk, is forced to apologise and then to drink his milk. At the end of the play the married neighbours are reconciled, and leave the house together:

LUCY

All right. Off you go, both of you.

ROSEMARY: *(kissing her on the cheek)*

Night night.

LUCY

Night, night dear. Night, night Terry.

TERRY *(kissing LUCY likewise)*

Night night.

LUCY

Sleep tight.

TERRY

Hope the bed bugs don't bite.

LUCY

Hold Rosemary's hand, Terry.

ROSEMARY and TERRY hold hands

See her home safely.

TERRY

Night.

ROSEMARY

Night.

LUCY

Night night.

TERRY and ROSEMARY go off hand in hand

LUCY blows kisses

(with a sigh) Blooming kids. Honestly.

So ends an exhilarating, and (when you see it in performance) surprisingly realistic, analysis of how 'behaviour breeds behaviour' – with a lesson, perhaps, that if you act like a child then you deserve to be treated like one. Child, parent, adult – the words you use set the tone for the way in which you develop relationships with those around you.

When you're thinking about how to 'act' verbal status, hold on to the image of a seesaw. There are many more than three potential points of balance on a seesaw, and you can modify your respective positions on it by subtly changing the words you use. If you think for a moment about how you alter the way in which you talk to different people in your life, then you'll surely know what I mean.

Actually, I don't know if you'll know what I mean, because we've probably never met. If I'd written 'you might know what I mean', which is nearer the mark, then you might feel mildly insulted at my implied criticism of your ability to follow my point. If I'd put 'you'll probably still be totally clueless as to what I'm on about', then the surprise you'd experience on reading these words might lead you to abandon the book entirely (or read on more intently!).

Which brings us (I hope) to an enjoyable complication in the game of verbal status: humour. If we have indeed met – if we are in fact friends – then you won't mind me poking fun at your status as a reader (you can't help struggling with these concepts, can you? Try reading it all again s-l-o-w-l-y). And you can call my book a heap of turgid, self-indulgent cowdung (probably). Friends allow each other to flout the rules of verbal status, and they use humour as the weapon.

Acting tip

The tantalising thing about all this for an actor, is that much of the detail of this stuff can't be known until rehearsal begins. One character fires an insult at another character. Is it a serious insult? Is it a joke which both enjoy? Or is it a clumsy attempt at humour which only one side finds funny? Part of the joy of rehearsal is to find out what's really going on. So come prepared to offer your director, and your fellow actors, more than one choice of intention to explore.

Exercises: Solo

Solo work on verbal status is, naturally, mostly limited to speech study or scene study. There's some fun and learning to be had, though, by exploring verbal status with people who are unwitting:

1) When you're next in a shop, offer a polite and genuine compliment to the assistant on some aspect of their appearance

(e.g. their choice of clothing). Watch their reaction carefully as they feel themselves raised on the seesaw.

2) On the next occasion, criticise yourself in some way (e.g. say 'I'm far too fat for this' when trying on a jacket; if they don't comment, add, 'I am, aren't I?'). Note the assistant's reaction.

3) When you next meet an acquaintance (someone who has not read this book!), offer them a huge compliment, and at the same time deliver a huge insult to yourself. Note their reaction.

4) When you next meet a (really good) friend (again, someone who has not read this book), offer them a big insult, and at the same time deliver a huge compliment to yourself. Note their reaction – and then tell them what you were doing. (Good luck with the friendship.)

Exercises: Partnered

1) Stand facing your partner. Compliment them on something which you genuinely find impressive – something about their appearance, or an aspect of their personality. Begin with the simple phrase 'Something I really like about you is – '. Your partner now takes a turn and compliments you. Keep the compliments going, and keep them brief. When you start to run out of things to say, break off and discuss how it felt to receive straightforward compliments.

2) As before. This time, insult each other with a comment about the other person's appearance or personality. Don't get too personal! If you're worried that the other person will take serious offence, limit the intensity of your insults (e.g. 'you talk too much'). An even less offensive version of this exercise involves using 'gobbledegook' insults – if you tell someone they smell like a dribbetefidgit it somehow feels less offensive! Afterwards, discuss how it felt to receive such insults.

3) As before, but this time offer your partner a barbed compliment which is really a coded insult. You might tell them,

'you do make the best of your hair', or 'you don't look anything like as old as you are', or 'you don't let go when you
know you're right about something'. Discuss how it felt to
be on the receiving end.

4) Set up a short 'Master and Servant' improvisation. The
servant has to deliver status-lowering insults without the
master fully realising what's going on. (A valet helping to
choose his master's shoes might ask, 'Sir, would you like the
old shoes, or the very old shoes?').

5) Conduct a scene-study in which you and a partner identify
words and phrases which seem to lower or raise the other
person's status. Run the scene with differing intentions:
first, perform it with all compliments and insults genuinely
felt. Next, perform it as though the two characters are
friends having a laugh: this time, all compliments are
jokingly insincere, and all insults are meant in fun.

In each case, discuss how the activity within each exercise alters
the relationship between the two partners, or the two characters.

Physical status

After I've known my acting students for a few weeks, I play a
trick on them. I call a routine break, then return to class. On my
return I ask the students to sit on the floor, and then I pick out
individuals in turn, politely inviting their comments on the
subject we were working on before the break. As soon as the class
gets underway, the students start to tense up. Normally extrovert
people begin to lower their heads and hope they won't be picked
on to speak. Class jokers stop joking. As I listen to people's
faltering comments, bolder individuals catch my eye but quickly
look away. Within ten minutes there is silence in the room, and a
pall of gloom.

At this point I can bear it no longer and admit to the students
that I've been role-playing. I ask them how they've been feeling
about me since we came back from the break. Each student was
feeling that I was annoyed or upset at them for something. Late

arrivals thought they were being cold-shouldered for poor time-keeping; jokers thought I'd found their jokes offensive; speakers had thought they were boring me. I ask them to identify what I'd been doing differently: they tell me I was being aggressive, or emotional, or unemotional. I ask them not to try to interpret my feelings, but to identify what I had actually been *doing* differently: what was I doing physically, that was different from my normal behaviour?

With questioning and encouragement, the students begin to identify that my physical behaviour had been temporarily altered. Where I would normally have sat at the same level as the group, this time I had stayed standing. I would normally have moved my eye contact around the group, but this time I'd either stared fixedly at an individual, or had looked away entirely. I would normally have fidgeted a bit – this time I'd kept very still. These, and other subtle changes in my physical behaviour, had unsettled them, and had altered the whole 'feel' of our relationship.

In status terms, I had taken on all the characteristics of high physical status. I'd been physically relaxed, but tall; I'd kept my hands on my hips, keeping myself open and so claiming a larger-than-normal physical space; I'd used dominant eye contact, but had offered no supporting behaviour (I didn't nod and smile to encourage speakers to continue). At one or two points I'd moved right up close to individual students, invading their personal space.

You can guess pretty well what signs I would have exhibited if I had been using very low-status physical behaviour. Physical conduct matters hugely in human interaction. In Section Three – The Body – we'll explore this in much more detail. As to exercises, the exploration of physical status is, of course, exploration of body language. The detailed exercises in the next Section will allow you to put these ideas on physical status into practice.

When you pull together the three types of status which a person uses – social, verbal and physical – you'll have a pretty sophisticated understanding of that person, and of your feelings towards them. As part of your acting planning, it can be useful to represent your status relationship with another character as a sort of a snapshot. And the 'seesaw' image is a particularly strong yet simple one to use. In the bottom-right section of the Character Profile Sheet, you'll see the title '**Status**'. Follow the guidelines in the section in the Appendix to show a key status relationship with another character.

Example: Natasha from *Three Sisters*

When you're filling in the 'seesaw' section of a Character Profile Sheet, you're effectively drawing together your sense of your character's overall status – social, verbal and physical – in relation to another key character. Masha makes a useful seesaw partner for Natasha, partly because Masha seems pretty outspoken in her criticism of her brother's wife. When you pull together the facts, the things Natasha has heard Masha say, and the snapshot we have of Natasha's personality, it seems likely that Natasha will feel herself strongly inferior to the sophisticated, outspoken Masha. The fact that Natasha is in charge of the running of the house in which Masha lives, becomes, therefore, an interesting complication.

Tool No. 3: Power Matters

The possession of power gives us confidence in dealing with other people. It brings with it status, and gives us something definite to negotiate with in everyday life.

Playwrights and actors understand about power, but their knowledge is usually instinctive rather than researched. Power is at the very heart of storytelling. King Lear's tragedy is that of a man who gives away power to people who want more, and who in the end take it all from him. The plays of Harold Pinter and Arthur Miller often play explicitly with power, and its uses and abuses, for their central conflicts. But what is power, and how can you define it?

Within business training, managers are often taught about power in all its glory, thanks to the work of researchers such as John R P French Jr and Bertram Raven. In a section of D Cartwright & A Zander's *Group Dynamics: Research and Theory* (Tavistock Publications, 1968) they describe several separately identifiable types of power. For me these boil down to:

1) *Agreed power* – power which a person is allowed to use as a result of their position within a culture (e.g. a manager can ask a junior member of a team to carry out a duty; a police officer is allowed to arrest a suspect; a parent can stop a child's pocket money as a punishment).

2) *Abuse power* – power which a person uses to force another person to do something (e.g. a school bully threatens another child unless dinner money is handed over). Abuse power is also used when a person with Agreed power abuses their authority (e.g. a doctor inappropriately asks a patient to strip).

3) *Reward power* – the power to supply something which is valued by another person (e.g. an interviewer rewards a candidate with a job; a parent rewards a child with a sweet; a child rewards a parent with a smile).

4) *Knowledge power* – power which comes from having information or expertise which is needed by someone else (e.g. a homeless person knows the location of the nearest taxi rank; a technician is able to repair a computer problem).

5) *Connection power* – power which comes from being close to someone who has power (e.g. a school pupil is the daughter of the headmaster; you have a friend who is a famous film actor).

6) *Personal power* – power which comes from a person's attractiveness to others, because of their looks or their personality (e.g. a model; a member of a group who can tell jokes brilliantly).

Here's an example of power at work. In this scenario I've marked, with the appropriate numbers, which power types are being used at each point in the story. There's a least one example of each type of power.

A park keeper sees a homeless male youth sleeping on a park bench in a city centre. The park keeper wakes the youth and orders him to move on (1): the youth gets up and shuffles away. The youth meets a pretty (6) female tourist, an off-duty policewoman, who asks him the way to the cathedral; they chat, and he gives precise instructions (4). As they part, the woman offers the youth some loose change (3): he takes it. The park keeper has been watching. As the woman starts to leave he goes over to the youth and demands the money, threatening to report him for begging (2). The youth calls out to the woman (5), and she returns and intervenes, showing her warrant card (1). The park keeper leaves quickly.

A person's power, then, derives from a variety of sources. Job, family role, education, skills developed (including for a hobby), personality, social class – all provide your character with aspects of power which gives them potential influence over others. Films, plays and television comedies are quite often built around a central misunderstanding regarding power: Nickolai Gogol's *The Government Inspector* (1836) stands as a shining example, a play in which a simple misunderstanding – the belief that a new arrival in town is an all-important government inspector, when in fact he's nothing of the sort – leads to a catalogue of incidents and accidents which reveal the darker side of town life. A whole episode of the classic TV comedy *Fawlty Towers* revolves around the mistaken belief that a customer is a top restaurant critic. But perhaps the best movie exploration of mistaken power takes place in the film *Being There*. An ageing and mentally subnormal gardener (Peter Sellers), thrust blinking into the modern world after the death of his employer, is run over and then nursed by a wealthy friend of the US President. His social shyness, and his randomly spoken advice on how to help plants grow, leads his all-powerful new friends to adopt him as a brilliant business guru who speaks in metaphors.

Willy Russell's *Blood Brothers* also takes an overt look at power – specifically, how access to power gives people advantages in life. Russell starts with a scenario in which twins from a poor background are separated at birth. While one twin, Mickey, remains with his mother, a cleaner, the other, Edward, is adopted into a wealthy home (where their mother has been working as their cleaner). We follow the twins' dramatic changes in fortune as they grow up, coming together infrequently, as they do, so that we (and they) can see the widening gulf between them.

Power issues are often most significant when you are on the receiving end of someone's else's power, and Willy Russell offers many examples of how society can favour those who are already advantaged in some way, whether it be within the fields of education, employment, health or social confidence. An early incident in Act One stands as an example of how someone with Agreed power uses it selectively – edging towards Abuse power in the first instance, and even offering the power to Reward, in the form of advice from someone who knows, in the second. Both twins have been caught red-handed on the point of committing a petty crime. To Mickey's mother he barks:

> Well, there'll be no more bloody warnings from now on. Either you keep them in order, Missis, or it'll be the courts for you, or worse, won't it?

To Edward's adoptive mother he says:

> An' er, as I say, it was more of a prank really, Mrs. Lyons. I'd just dock his pocket money if I was you. *(Laughs)* But one thing I would say, if y'don't mind me sayin', is, well, I'm not sure I'd let him mix with the likes of them in the future. Make sure he keeps with his own kind, Mrs. Lyons.

Russell uses the narrative of his musical play to argue persuasively that if we use our various powers to treat people in radically different ways – praising one while chastising the other, favouring one while disadvantaging the other, and so on – then we are, each of us, complicit in influencing the way people turn out.

Acting tips

Once you're aware of the importance of different types of power, you can start to use that knowledge to sharpen your sensitivity onstage. As part of the planning stage of acting, you should comb through your script to work out which types of power your character possesses. You can list these for quick reference in the **Power** section of your Character Profile Sheet.

For an actor, awareness of power can really help to clarify why your character behaves the way he does, and why others allow him to do so. It can also help you to avoid stereotyping. A character with low social status, such as a prostitute, may have an abundance of certain power types: Personal (being good-looking); knowledge (of street life, and clients' names); Connection (with their pimp, and with important clients); Abuse (threatening to reveal clients' names); and Reward (use your imagination!). Likewise, a character with apparent high social status – the ceremonial mayor of a town, for example – may in truth have very little influence over others.

Exercises: Solo

1) Draw up a list of powers which you personally possess. Be imaginative! – if you're unemployed you are still likely to have the Agreed power to demand payment of benefit within a certain time period. Come up with at least one example, per power category, of occasions on which you've exercised each of these powers over someone else.

2) Think of someone you know well, who doesn't strike you as being particularly powerful. List the six power types. Now try to come up with at least one example per power 'category'. (A person's expert knowledge of *Star Wars* figures might not impress you personally, but ...)

3) Select from a published play a monologue which requires you to speak to an onstage character. Comb through the speech for moments at which your character seems to be using a specific type of power to influence the other person. Identify the power 'type' being used in each case.

Exercises: Partnered

1) Choose a frozen moment from an imaginary scene in which two power 'types' have momentarily come together in conflict. For example, a parent is about to use Abuse power to strike a child, while the child is trying to deflect punishment with Personal power via a friendly pleading expression; or, a headteacher is trying to use Agreed power to refuse admission to the child of a 'pushy' parent, who is offering to write a cheque for school funds. Don't plan the scene, but on a cue unfreeze the action and see what happens. Try removing one of the power bases (e.g. the parent has no spare funds) and see what happens this time. Then try adding some new power to one of the characters.

2) Similar to 3) in the solo exercises above. Select a duologue from a published play. Comb through the scene for moments at which each character seems to be using a specific type of power to influence the other; identify the power 'type' being used in each case. Run the scene with a keen awareness of what powers are being used.

3) As above, but this time discuss with your partner some sort of shift in power – e.g. if A previously found B very attractive (i.e. B has Personal power), this time B is considered less attractive. Or (taking the imaginary example from 1) above), a parent wanting to use Abuse power against his child is wheelchair-bound. Re-run the scene and discuss how the dynamics have changed, even though the scripted lines remain the same.

Example: Natasha from *Three Sisters*

Chekhov has endowed Natasha with a fascinatingly comprehensive range of powers, which, when lined up alongside the powers of Andrei and his sisters, should suggest to us why his play is less a drama of inaction (a common criticism of *Three Sisters*), and more a drama of what powerful people suffer when they find themselves restrained by society, and by their own personalities. Natasha is accorded considerable Agreed power through her marriage to Andrei – over the servants, for example, and to a lesser degree over her sisters-in-law. She feels justified in sliding over into Abuse power when she loses her temper, at both servants and sisters. She enjoys her Reward power over both Andrei and the children, indulging the latter with comfort (including Irina's room) and attention. As a member of the household she no doubt collects valuable Knowledge power over those around her, but her particular expertise seems to derive from her role as a mother (something only she among the four women enjoys). Her Connection power to Andrei, and by association to the sisters, brings her status within the local community. And her beauty is a source of Personal power over both Andrei, and later, over Protopopov (no doubt among others). So someone who seems at first reading to be something of an outsider and a victim, starts to seem altogether more interesting.

section 3: **the body**

In this Section we will be concentrating on how actors, and indeed people in everyday life, use their bodies to communicate things to others. You will be introduced to five new Tools which allow you to change the way in which you express yourself through your body.

Actors use their knowledge of non-verbal communication to ensure that accurate and appropriate messages reach their audience. When you are onstage or on screen, you should be at least partly aware of how your body is communicating things, so that you can make adjustments if your communication is somehow 'wrong'. This Section gives you the knowledge you need to achieve such awareness. Actors also use knowledge of physical behaviour to widen their 'range' – i.e. to play a wider cross-section of character types. The five new Tools in this Section will help you, too, become more versatile.

Tool Number 4 – Adjusting Tension – explores how muscle tension reflects a character's psychological state. Tool Number 5 – Adjusting Height – considers why people alter their height above and below their normal 'standing' height. Tool Number 6 – Adjusting Openness – examines how, by covering or exposing their chest and stomach, a person can reveal their thoughts and feelings. Tool Number 7 – Working on Eye Contact – explores the meanings behind differing levels and durations of eye contact. And Tool Number 8 – Adjusting Space – assesses the way in which we handle physical space when we are with others.

As in the previous Section, you will be given examples, acting tips and exercises to allow you to develop your ability to change your physical behaviour in performance.

At the risk of stating the obvious, no-one can actually hear your thoughts. They're yours, and if you choose to keep them private, you can. People can (and will) guess at what is going on in your mind, but they're only guessing.

Some years ago, a police recruitment poster boasted that officers were trained to spot when a suspect was lying: the suspect would rub his nose when speaking. I imagine that one or two suspects went to court for having an itchy nose.

Of course, there are physical signs which even some of our greatest actors can't fake. Sweating, turning pale, going dry in the mouth – these require real psychological stimulus. Beyond these signs, we are as a species pretty good at throwing others off the scent – generally by controlling our animal impulses for fight or flight.

However, you can often get a sense of what is really going on in someone's mind. The secret is to keep an eye on what they can't control so well. Broadly speaking, the further away from the face you go, the more revealing the clues are likely to be. A twitch of a finger or foot can say something really important about the mood of person (experts call a sign such as a twitch, 'leakage'). These, and other aspects of the behaviour of the human animal (you could call him the 'humanimal'), have been comprehensively and fascinatingly explored by experts such as zoologist Desmond Morris (see Further Reading).

For the actor who wants to be really versatile – who wants to portray the widest possible range of different types of human behaviour – what does he need to know? What are the key 'variables' in the body, that alter according to someone's personality? There are five – or, at least, four plus a joker in the pack. The variables are **T**ension, **H**eight, **O**penness, **S**pace (or rather use of space) and **E**ye contact; together they form the mnemonic **THOSE**. Space is the joker, as you'll see.

Tool No. 4: Adjusting Tension

Tension occurs when you contract muscles: they tighten. Often this is for some necessary reason: you want to pick up an object, to move forwards, or simply to avoid falling over. Just standing still demands some muscle tension. Frequently, though, we use muscles without any such necessary reason. As a result of some psychological stimulus, we become 'tense'.

One stereotype of a very tense person is a regimental sergeant-major in the army. In charge of a gang of undisciplined young conscripts, he must knock them into shape in time for inspection by a senior officer. At stake is the reputation both of the regiment, and of the sergeant-major as a disciplinarian. He stands ramrod-straight in front of his new charges.

One of the new recruits represents the sergeant-major's biggest challenge, and is his opposite in terms of physical tension. A hippy, used to resting and sleeping when and where he feels like it, he is at ease with the world and sees no need to waste energy on pointless drilling. His favourite position is flat on his back, marijuana joint in hand, contemplating the cosmos. The stage is set for conflict ...

Extreme opposites are, then, easy to recognise; but tension in people normally takes more subtle forms. Among the guests at a showbiz party are two people facing one another. The first, a man, is standing and, although he has no need to move, his body is tense: his brow is knitted, he has slightly lifted shoulders, his stomach is tight, fists and buttocks partially clenched, kneecaps pulled upwards, even his toes are clawed inside his shoes. The woman he speaks to is standing too, but she uses pretty well only the muscles she needs. There's some tension in her face – she is smiling at the man as he talks – but otherwise her body has only enough tension to allow her to stand, and to hold her drink.

In the animal world, tension acts as a state of readiness for 'fight or flight'. The need to be ready to stay and fight, or to suddenly flee, is most common in animals which are lower down the food chain – the hunted. Birds and mice are good examples, and they have a metabolism to match: racing heartbeat, sudden, twitchy movements, always on the lookout for trouble. Conversely, the creatures which can relax the most are the ones which are hunted least: the hunters. Think of lions basking in the sun. They feel no threat, so need not be on constant lookout; they use tension only when needed and with economy, perhaps when sauntering to the lake for a drink. Even when hunting at full speed, much of the lion's body is untensed.

In human animals, mental state is likely to be the biggest factor in determining how tense, or how relaxed, a person is. Confidence develops, or fails to develop, partly in response to life experiences; and of course the degree of confidence you feel changes according to circumstances. Think of the couple at the party. Let's add a few facts to help explain the difference in physical tension in each of our two subjects.

The man is an actor fresh out of drama school. He considers himself a fairly shy person with strangers, though he knows he can be totally extrovert with his friends. He really only came to the party because an actor-friend said that some influential people might be there. He doesn't want to be thought of as lacking ambition, but right now he feels out of place and would much sooner slip off home.

The woman he is speaking to is a television casting director. Successful in her work, she prides herself on being friendly and approachable, despite the power she exerts in her job. She is a skilled questioner, and has decided to find out more about this man. She is confident, in control, and happy to be doing what she is doing. The man, though, is suffering a conflict: his animal instincts are telling him to retreat, but his mind is telling him he must stay and be sociable with this woman. Result: he is tense, she is relaxed.

Of course it's not quite that straightforward. Though she's not aware of it, the woman has some unnecessary tension in her jaw, and in her right foot. She is finding conversation with the man hard work, and has picked up on his unease. As she listens, she is also mentally scripting her polite exit from this situation.

Acting tips

Tension is the enemy of effective performance: it strangles vocal resonance, and inhibits physical spontaneity. Before you can use tension effectively as an actor, you need to be able to relax at the drop of a hat. A painter needs a blank canvas for his work; he creates from there. A fully relaxed body is the actor's blank canvas; he creates from that.

The actor in performance should use added tension with care. The voice is especially susceptible to damage from tension, so try to avoid, even when playing a very tense character, centering your character's stress in the throat or neck. There are other ways to reveal mental unease, for example through slight tensing of more visible parts of the body such as your fingers and feet, or through other means such as vocal changes (the note of the voice may be higher than usual, for example). Of course with practice and training you shouldn't need to be thinking about such things in performance; but while you're still developing control over your body 'signs', such awareness is valuable.

Exercises: Solo

1) Practise relaxing your body as fully as you can, lying flat on the floor. Tense and then relax each set of muscles in your body, starting with the toes and working through to your face. Try to breathe normally as you tense and relax. You might find it useful to learn or record the words in the Appendix as mentioned earlier, 'Relaxation Exercise with Visualisation'.

2) Practise relaxing your body as fully as you can, standing.

3) Select a specific point in your body. Tense that point, and move around with that point still tensed. Make a mental note of how the tensing of that point affects you. Add one or two other points of tension, and note how your brain starts to engage with your bodily stress: your mind is looking to justify the stress in a rational way, perhaps by suggesting a reason for being uncomfortable.

4) Observe people's points of tension at any social gathering.

Notice unnecessary tension in people's bodies, and ask yourself what might motivate it. Try imitating their tension. Be imaginative!

Exercises: Partnered

1) Using a scale of one to ten, you and your partner should each choose a level of confidence in social situations: ten is high, five medium, one is low. Create a 'back story' to support your feelings. Enter a set situation when ready, maintaining an appropriate degree of tension. Stay aware of your tension in the scene, but behave as truthfully as you can.

2) Two people are talking. One (a tense person) wants to get away; the other (a relaxed person) is happy to stay talking. The tense person in fact seems relaxed, but subtly 'leaks' tension, e.g. nodding more than necessary, rubbing fingers together, smiling fixedly. Choose a location, and two characters – and decide why the first one is tense, and the other relaxed. Again, stay aware of your tension in the scene, but behave as truthfully as you can.

Example: Natasha from *Three Sisters*

Read and rehearse the scene below from Act One, in which we first meet Natasha. Pay close attention to how the psychological pressure she experiences as a result of being 'on show', and of having made a 'wrong' choice of what to wear, might show itself through hidden tension:

[Enter NATALIA IVANOVNA; she wears a pink dress and a green sash.]

NATASHA

They're already at lunch ... I'm late ... *[Examines herself in the mirror, composes herself]* I think my hair's not too bad ... *[Sees IRINA]* Dear Irina Sergeyevna, congratulations! *[Kisses her firmly]* You've so many guests, I'm really embarrassed ... How do you do, Baron!

OLGA *[Enters from dining-room]*
    And here's Natasha. How are you, dear!

    [They embrace.]

NATASHA
    Happy Name Day to Irina! I feel awfully shy, there's so many people here.

OLGA
    It's just our friends. *[Alarmed, in an undertone]* You're wearing a green sash! My dear, you shouldn't!

NATASHA
    Is it bad luck?

OLGA
    No, it simply doesn't match ... and it looks odd.

NATASHA *[In a tearful voice]*
    Really? But it isn't really green, it's more – neutral.

    [Goes into dining-room with OLGA.]

Tool No. 5: Adjusting Height

We all achieve a natural height in adulthood. This of course is something we cannot control, being set as it is by things such as genes and nutrition. But whatever height you happen to be, you alter it on a moment-by-moment basis. Often the changes in height are subtle, but they can be big and decisive. At times your decision to change height will be driven by a need for comfort, such as straightening your spine when sat at a keyboard for a long time. But you will also often raise or lower your body beyond what is strictly necessary. Why?

People alter their height in order to claim a particular position on the status 'seesaw'. Picture the following stereotypical scene in a 'posh' restaurant:

A young man, a first-time diner in this sort of establishment, has brought his girlfriend here, partly to impress her. He wants to seem confident and in control, but he now feels out of his depth: he's not sure of the rules of etiquette and he fears looking foolish. He's being attended to by a waiter who privately disapproves of the young man and his 'type': at first glance the waiter could tell that the diner is in unfamiliar surroundings – he is slightly hunched, as if he doesn't want to be noticed. The waiter likes to reflect the status and reputation of the restaurant, so he holds himself in a raised but relaxed posture, with his head tipped back very slightly. When he first speaks to the young diner, the waiter's posture leaves the diner with the distinct impression that the waiter is 'talking down his nose' at him, despite the apparently friendly tone of the waiter's voice.

In the animal world, changes in height take place for solid practical reasons which have everything to do with survival. The hunter finds a position of height from which to seek prey; think of an eagle wheeling high above oblivious creatures on the ground. The hunted also use increased height at times to scour the horizon for threats – think of a meerkat at full stretch. Both hunter and hunted also lower their height for practical reasons: picture a cat stalking a bird, the cat's whole body is kept low in order to be unseen. Picture too the reaction of a squirrel when it hears something threatening: it drops in height and freezes.

'Humanimals' – people – tend to alter their height in company. This often occurs when a person's job requires them to think about how they influence others. A police detective may remain standing when aggressively interrogating a suspect who is seated, in order to press for a confession; a counsellor working with a child may sit on the floor to seem less threatening, and so encourage the child to speak.

People also alter their height in relation to others in social situations. A high-status player in the company of someone who is seated normally may sit on the arm of a chair; they prefer to 'look down on' others. A low-status player will tend to reduce their relative height – they prefer to 'look up to' others. Within a group of friends, there will usually be someone who prefers the floor or a beanbag to a place on the sofa.

Sometimes people claim height (and so higher status) as a way of masking their own lack of confidence: they feel more in control, if they are higher up than the other person. Think back to the restaurant scene. This time the waiter's intention is to make the young man feel relaxed and welcome. Meanwhile the young man wants to be more convincingly at ease. The waiter retains his formal body height, which he feels is respectful to the diner – he is after all 'on duty'. He does not however tilt his head upwards, but keeps it level and relaxed. The young man avoids slouching and instead holds a more upright posture. But in truth he is sitting a little too upright to seem relaxed and comfortable.

My local pizza restaurant – part of a national chain – experimented recently with the height 'issue' in relation to customers. Waiting staff would make a point of sitting down at the table with you to take your order. It was an interesting tactic: for me it felt more informal, more friendly, a discussion rather than a formal interaction. It did, though, require the waiter to enter your 'personal space' – your table – not something people are used to in restaurants. And not all waiting staff managed the 'friendly' bit well. After about a month the policy was quietly dropped.

Acting tips

As with tension, height in performance is something which needs to be handled sensibly. If you stretch yourself too high, or if you compress yourself too much, you will be adding tension which may harm your performance, especially your vocal performance.

The 'extremes' of use of height in performance are probably best reserved for broad comedy, or for heightened drama such as the plays of the Restoration period. In everyday life we tend to be pretty subtle when changing height.

It's often valuable to see what happens if you try 'doing the opposite'. Let's say that in rehearsal you're perched on the arm of a sofa in a scene with another actor who is standing. Your characters are arguing. You feel the need to rise and face the other actor, which would mean standing to match their height. Try instead sliding down from the arm onto the seat of the sofa: the resulting change in mood, driven perhaps by your character's desire to seem unthreatened, may form a more interesting and truthful choice.

Exercises: Solo

1) When out shopping, move around with your height raised above what is normal for you. Make a mental note of how the change affects you. Note how your brain starts to engage with the change: your mind is looking to justify it – perhaps you start to feel more powerful, even a bit pompous. Try doing the opposite. Note whether other people's reactions to you change at all.

2) Observe people's use of height at a social gathering. Notice unnecessary changes in height, and ask yourself what might motivate them. Imitate them. Be imaginative!

3) Select a short audition monologue you know well – one in which you are talking directly to someone else. Restage it, subtly altering your height at points where it seems psychologically appropriate. At times you may change height because you feel in control; at other times, you change height because you're less confident. Changes in height should be fluid, subtle and responsive. Ask an observer to watch your revised performance: chances are, the invisible onstage character you are addressing will become more 'visible' to your observer.

Exercises: Partnered

1) Think of a formal work situation in which people will often consciously alter their height when meeting and talking. Rehearse, and then perform, a short scene which shows this. Find out how it feels if the heights are reversed.

2) Think of a social situation where, because of their confidence levels, people may alter their height when meeting and talking. Rehearse, and then perform a short scene which shows this. Find out how it feels if the heights are reversed.

Example: Natasha from *Three Sisters*

Read and rehearse the section of a scene below from Act One, which follows moments after the previous scene (when we first met Natasha). Pay close attention to how the psychological pressure Natasha experiences as a result of feeling ridiculed, might show itself through changed height:

[Loud laughter; NATASHA rushes out into the sitting-room, followed by ANDREI]

ANDREI

Pay no attention to them! Wait ... stop, please. ...

NATASHA

I'm so ashamed ... I don't know what's the matter with me, they're all laughing at me. It wasn't nice of me to leave the table, but I can't help it ... I can't. *[Covers her face with her hands.]*

ANDREI

Please, dear, don't be upset. They're only joking, they're kind people. My dear, darling Natasha, they're all kind and good people, and they love us both. Come to the window, they can't see us here ... *[Looks round.]*

NATASHA

I'm just not used to company.

ANDREI

Oh you're so young, so beautiful, so wonderful! My darling, don't be upset! Believe me, believe me ... I'm so happy, my heart is full of love, of ecstasy ... They can't see us! They can't! How I've fallen in love with you – Oh, I don't know anything. My dear, pure darling, be my wife! I love you, love you as I've never loved before ... *[They kiss.]*

[Two officers come in and, seeing the lovers kiss, stop in astonishment.]

Tool No. 6: Adjusting Openness

Openness describes the degree of exposure or concealment of the front of the body. 'Fully open' would mean that your legs are apart, your head is raised slightly to expose your neck, and your arms are away from your torso, for example with your hands on hips; or, if you're seated, your hands may be joined behind your head with fingers interlocked. 'Fully closed' would leave you with your legs entwined, your head tilted down, and your arms folded tightly across chest or stomach. The degree of openness is one of the most influential bodily signs; you can make a strong initial judgement on a person's state of mind by looking at their openness from some distance away.

Animals' degree of openness tends to reveal how vulnerable they feel to attack by hunters. The ultimate degree of concealment and self-protection – the favoured defence posture among many animals – is the 'foetal' position. Others instinctively make themselves as small and low as possible, using the ground as part of their protective shield: think of a mouse caught out in the open. Under intense physical threat humanimals may do either; significantly, they will also show a defensive physical response as a result of psychological, and not just physical, threat.

So a humanimal's degree of openness or concealment gives real clues to his mental state. The posture adopted tends to reflect a person's degree of confidence, and their sense of status relative to others present. Let's start with the stereotypes. Picture a poolside scene: a super-confident and well-muscled lifeguard is chatting up (and being chatted up by) a shy bather, who is wearing her new bikini for the first time. He'll probably have his hands on his hips, she'll probably have her arms folded in front of her. His legs will be apart in 'on duty' mode; hers probably slightly crossed if standing, tightly entwined if she is sat. He is exposing his body shape, suggesting that he is unconcerned about threat; she is partially hiding hers, projecting her vulnerability, inviting him, to follow the cliché, to protect her.

Of course it's rarely as straightforward as that. Sophisticated as we humanimals are, we tend to be aware of what potential signals we're giving out, so we throw in a few big distractions. Time for a bit of role-reversal. Back to our couple at the poolside: let's add a few new bits of information. He is a little unconfident about his physique (not uncommon these days among bodybuilders – the so-called Adonis syndrome). She knows she looks fabulous in her new bikini. He finds her perceived superconfidence a bit too much – he prefers to feel in control in this developing relationship. She wants to know if he has the personality to match the body; she is struggling to get conversation out of him and is rapidly losing interest. He, lost for words, pretends that he is being super-vigilant at the poolside in case of any accidents. Both wish they could say something funny to lighten the mood, but nothing appropriate is coming to mind.

How might this new information show itself in their relative body postures? He, 'on duty' and on show, probably tries to maintain a degree of openness – legs apart, head up – but folds his arms over his chest to shore up his confidence (and make his biceps look bigger!). Surprised at her lack of progress, she has dropped her head slightly. Her legs are uncrossed and her hands are on her hips, but she is starting to feel exposed. Just after he has folded his arms she does the same, partially mirroring his posture (so-called postural echo). This feels instinctively more comfortable, and gives one of them the confidence to risk a joke.

Contradictory signs – such as arms folded but legs apart – are a common part of people's interpersonal armoury: it throws the other person 'off the scent' and prevents them from reading a person's true feelings. But we humanimals are cleverer still: we commonly use inanimate objects to justify the degree of our openness or concealment.

One final visit to the poolside. Things are not going too well, and she is about to make her exit – unaware that he is too. Each has one or two items: he has his lifeguard's whistle and wears sunglasses; she has a small shoulder bag, sunglasses resting on her head, and a towel draped around her shoulders. Earlier in the meeting she had lightly towel-dried her hair, requiring her to raise her arms and expose her chest. Keen now for an exit she has pulled the towel protectively around her shoulders. She has also dropped her sunglasses down over her eyes. Using both hands he adjusts his sunglasses on his head, giving him an opening-up gesture which subtly increases his sense of confidence. He also puts the whistle in his mouth, supposedly in reaction to a bit of splashing going on in the pool, but in truth to excuse himself from the effort of making further conversation. She fishes in her bag for some loose change and, finding it, looks purposely in the direction of the poolside bar. After a few moments, and with little more than a nod and a smile from each of them, he toots briefly on his whistle and moves towards the pool, while she moves off to the bar.

Acting tips

Most types of openness or protective behaviour will cause no harm to your technical acting performance, though a really closed posture is going to reduce both your vocal resonance and your available breath. It's worth getting really familiar with this aspect of body language – it's one of the most instinctive, so, when used sensitively in a scene with another actor, it can really help a scene to seem 'real'. It's common for two people to shift postural openness in direct response to one another, and this tends to be very fluid: if you're tense onstage or on set, you run the risk of being 'left behind' when your fellow actor shifts his degree of openness or concealment. A shift in openness can also offer an audience vital clues to your character's attitude towards a new arrival in the scene.

Exercises: Solo

1) Next time you find yourself under pressure in a public situation – at a party, for example – take note of your bodily openness. If you find you have closed up in some way, try adopting a clear open posture, e.g. hands on hips. Maintain this for some time and see how it affects your own feelings. Note also whether other people alter their behaviour towards you.

2) Choose a modern naturalistic monologue you are comfortable with, which you know well, and which is delivered to an unseen onstage character. Restage it, using your full knowledge of openness. Subtly use one or two appropriate small props in your self-redirection.

Exercises: Partnered

1) Openness in a human animal gives clues to the character's mental state; the amount of openness can reveal a person's confidence, and their sense of relative status. There may be hidden thoughts or feelings which 'leak out'. Think of a situation in which two people might meet. Using a scale of one to ten, choose a level of confidence for each of you: one is low, five is medium, ten is high. Create a 'back story' to support your behaviour. Enter the set situation when you're ready, and behave as truthfully as you can. Stay aware of your openness during the scene.

2) A person may use openness to manipulate the reactions of others, e.g. pretending to be vulnerable in order to be chatted up at a party by a 'hunter'; pretending to be tough in a dangerous neighbourhood. Think of a situation in which this sort of need might arise when two people meet. Using a scale of one to ten, choose a level of confidence. Create a

'back story' to support your behaviour. Before the scene begins, take on the character's normal, 'real' openness. Then adopt the 'pretend openness' which is designed to manipulate the feelings and behaviour of the other person. Enter the set situation when you're ready. Concentrate on staying aware of the mental conflict in maintaining the 'adopted' openness during the scene.

3) People often make subtle use of objects when interacting with others. These can help boost confidence, or can hide real feelings. Select some small items for possible use, e.g. bag, newspaper, mobile phone, mirror, glasses. Prepare as before, but use the items subtly during the scene to help you become more open, or more concealed.

4) The degree of openness a person shows will be fluid and changing, depending on who they are with and how they are feeling. Openness reveals their sense of relative status. Think of a social situation in which two people meet. Plan a moment in your scene when something big changes the relative status between the two characters – e.g. a decision, or a revelation. Explore during the scene how openness alters in each character, before, during and after the 'moment'. Try running the scene as (a) strangers; (b) friends; (c) lovers.

Example: Natasha from *Three Sisters*

Read and rehearse the scene below from Act Two. Natasha, bearing a message, finds Andrei. Consider how she might use her talk of the cold (she seems to have banned fires in the house) as an excuse for maintaining the 'security blanket' of a closed posture. Perhaps when she mentions the entertainers she might open up a little as her sense of having some control returns – and again, as she plots to have Irina moved out of her room.

[Scene as before. It is 8 pm. Somebody is playing an accordian outside in the street. There is no light. NATALIA IVANOVNA enters in a dressing gown carrying a candle; she stops by the door which leads into ANDREI'S room.]

NATASHA

> What are you doing, Andrei? Are you reading? It's nothing, I just ...

[She opens another door, and looks in, then closes it]

> No candles lit ...

ANDREI *[Enters with book in hand]*
> What are you doing, Natasha?

NATASHA

> I was looking to see if there's any lights on. It's Shrovetide, and the servant is getting careless, I have to keep watch constantly. When I came through the dining-room yesterday at midnight, there was a candle still burning. I couldn't get her to say who lit it. *[Puts down her candle]* What's the time?

ANDREI *[Looks at his watch]*
> Quarter past eight.

NATASHA

> And Olga and Irina are still out. The poor things are still at work. Olga at the staff meeting, Irina at her telegraph office ... *[Sighs]* I said to your sister this morning, 'Irina, darling, you must look after yourself.' But she won't listen. Did you say quarter past eight? I'm afraid little Bobik is quite ill. Why is he so cold? He was feverish yesterday, but to-day he's freezing ... I'm so worried ...

ANDREI

> He's all right, Natasha. The boy is fine.

NATASHA

Still, I think we should check he's eating properly. I'm so worried. And the entertainers were to be here after nine; it's best they don't come, Andrei.

ANDREI

Well – I don't know. We did invite them.

NATASHA

This morning, when that little boy woke up and saw me he suddenly smiled; he knew me. 'Hello, Bobik!' I said, 'good morning, darling.' And he laughed. Children understand, they understand very well. So I'll tell them, Andrei dear, not to let the musicians in.

ANDREI *[Hesitatingly]*

Surely that's up to my sisters. This is their home.

NATASHA

I'll tell them. They're so kind ... *[Going]* I've ordered sour milk for supper. The doctor says you must eat sour milk and nothing else, or you'll never lose weight. *[Stops]* Bobik is so cold. I'm afraid his room is too cold for him. It would be nice to put him into another room till the warm weather comes. Irina's room, for instance, is just right for a baby: it's dry and it gets the sun all day. I must tell her, she can share Olga's room. She's not at home in the daytime, she only sleeps here ... *[A pause]* Andrei, darling, why so silent?

ANDREI

I was just thinking ... there's really nothing to say ...

NATASHA

Well ... there was something I wanted to tell you ... Oh, yes. Ferapont has come from the Council, he wants to see you.

ANDREI *[Yawns]*
  Call him here.

  [NATASHA goes out]

Tool No. 7: Working on Eye Contact

The eyes are the mirror to the soul, someone once said. And the eyes have it, when it comes to communication between people. We use them to 'read' other people, and to signal (or disguise) our own feelings and intentions.

What matters most is the direction, and the duration, of eye contact between people. The extreme opposites would of course be continuous eye contact, and no eye contact at all. Also of interest is 'flickered' eye contact, when people look up briefly but choose not to hold eye contact.

In the animal world, full eye contact from a hunter indicates high status: 'you look tasty', the animal might be thinking. But high status can also be claimed as a result of giving no eye contact, which might be interpreted as, 'you're not worth my attention'. Full eye contact from a creature which is hunted can also indicate readiness to flee: 'Is he still there?'. No eye contact from a hunted creature can also mean submission: 'I know you're the boss.' Flickered eye contact – looking up briefly, but always looking away first – can indicate acceptance of a lower status: 'Hello and all that, but I'm really no threat to you.' (Horse-whisperers use this technique.)

With humanimals, most of the time it's much the same. The main difference is, once again, that we routinely manipulate our behaviour for some hidden reason. One comic stereotype might be the old-fashioned headmaster in assembly, steering laser-beam eyes around the school hall in an attempt to spy potential trouble-makers. Under his fierce stare the pupils remain stock-still and resolutely refuse to catch his eye.

It's important to keep in mind the simple idea of hunter/hunted roles in the animal kingdom, as, so often, they find a parallel in human relationships. We humans still hunt, and are hunted; it's just that we no longer eat each other. Instead we hunt for status, for positions in relationships which provide us with a sense of comfort. And we do in this in a range of subtle, sophisticated, and at times seemingly contradictory ways.

We are, from an early age, aware of the use and effects of eye contact. But as we get older we become more sophisticated. A group of four-year-olds would show active disinterest in the company of a boring teacher, looking away, yawning, staring out of the window. A bored secondary school pupil might feign interest with occasional strong eye contact; a university student trapped in a dull lecture might well apply himself with apparent fervour to the task of note-taking.

Eye contact between people shows interest or respect (or a lack of it). Full eye contact can mean either a high-status sense of your being in control, or a low-status sense of you being controlled: blinking reduces your sense of power and control. Looking away first can show acceptance of lower status than that of the person who is looking at you; or it can imply that you're losing interest in that person. If you want to be confident that you have 'read' the meaning behind a person's eye contact – especially if you're observing one of these 'either/or' situations – look for the tension in the face and the body. A person who is most at ease with high-status behaviour will make strong choices with their eye contact, and will underpin this with a relaxed face and body.

Some interesting recent research explores how eye movement relates to mental recall, such as remembering events. Broadly speaking, if you're 'seeing' images in your mind, your eyes look upwards as if you are looking at the images on a raised screen in front of you. If you're recalling or hearing sounds, your eyes tend to move to the side. And if you're recalling or experiencing strong feelings, your eyes tend to move downwards. I think it's interesting for actors to explore this. Try to catch yourself when you are remembering things. And explore how the theory works with spontaneous experience, too: I've noticed that when I'm listening to someone on the phone, my eyes tend to move subtly but quickly from side to side. I think this sort of awareness of the subtleties of behaviour is really worth exploring; I know that some teachers believe it can harm your spontaneity, but in my experience, once you've developed an ease with such knowledge, it will simply make you a more resourceful, versatile and truthful actor.

Acting tips

How long would your character hold eye contact with another character? Don't worry about this in detail; there are too many variables to make a technically 'correct' answer in any particular circumstance. Just learn the theory, explore it in rehearsal, and then trust your instincts in performance. Your character's attempts to achieve his objective – his 'want' at any particular moment (see Section Six, 'Inner Life') – should keep your physical behaviour focused and appropriate.

Keep this in mind, though. Generally speaking, the better you know someone, the less you feel the need to give them regular eye contact. There's less need for you to supply them with visual signs, such as smiling and nodding, since you understand each other well and are unlikely to offend one another. Also, you will find yourself needing to look elsewhere in order to unearth the more personal thoughts and feelings that friends discuss. It's difficult to form complicated thoughts, or indeed to recall events, if you're looking straight into someone's eyes.

Exercises: Solo

1) Try altering your preferred use of eye contact for a day. If you tend to look away first, hold strong eye contact instead. Maintain this behaviour for some time and see how it affects your own feelings. Note also whether other people alter their behaviour towards you.

2) Choose a modern naturalistic monologue you're comfortable with and know well; select one in which there is another character in the scene, even though your audience cannot see them. Restage the monologue, using your full knowledge of the use of eye contact.

Exercises: Partnered

1) Think of a work-related situation in which a professional person may consciously alter their eye contact in relation to a customer or client. You can use previous examples if you wish, e.g. detective/suspect, counsellor/child. Devise a short scene which shows this.

2) Think of a social situation in which two people, recent acquaintances, meet, but one of them wants to hide their real feelings. Devise the scene so that eye contact is manipulated by that person, to throw the other 'off the scent'.

3) Think of a situation in which two close friends are seated facing outwards on a bench. Devise the scene so that the friends' level of eye contact reflects their level of familiarity. Run the scene again with almost constant eye contact; discuss the difference in the 'feel' of the relationship.

4) Practise chatting with your partner with differing degrees of eye contact. Discuss after how it is that different levels of eye contact affect your idea of what your partner is feeling towards you.

Example: Natasha from *Three Sisters*

Read and rehearse this longer scene below from Act Two. For the first time we see Natasha in the company of most of the men, including VERSHININ, BARON TUZENBACH, SOLENI, FEDOTIK (all army officers), and CHEBUTIKIN (an army doctor). MASHA and IRINA are also present, along with ANFISA, a servant.

This is a highly charged scene for Natasha; these important people are guests in her house. Her husband is absent from the room. If she is to compete with Masha and Irina for the attention of the men, she may be tempted to call on her Personal power as claimed through her beauty. Consider how she might use her eyes to do this. Soleni's snub will doubtless affect her confidence with eye contact, though she may want to hide this. Though she speaks little in the scene, her use of French to put down Masha at the end suggests that she is still working hard to impress.

[A samovar is brought in; ANFISA attends to it; a little later NATASHA enters and helps by the table; SOLENI arrives and, after greetings, sits by the table.]

VERSHININ

What a wind!

MASHA

Yes. I'm sick of winter. I've already forgotten what summer's like.

IRINA

The cards are coming out, I see. We're going to Moscow.

FEDOTIK

No, they're not. Look, the eight was on the two of spades. *[Laughs]* That means you won't be going to Moscow.

CHEBUTIKIN *[Reading paper]*

Tsitsigar. Smallpox is raging there.

ANFISA *[Coming up to MASHA]*

Masha, have some tea, my dear. *[To VERSHININ]* Please have some, sir ... excuse me, sir, but I've forgotten your name ...

MASHA

Bring some here, Nanny. I'm not going over there.

IRINA

Nanny!

ANFISA

Coming, coming!

NATASHA *[To SOLENI]*

Babies understand perfectly. I said 'Good morning, Bobik;

good morning, dear!' And he looked at me in a special way.
You think it's just the mother in me speaking; I assure you
that it's not! He's a wonderful child.

SOLENI

If he was my child I'd roast him on a frying-pan and eat him.
[Takes his tumbler into the drawing-room and sits in a corner.]

NATASHA *[Covers her face in her hands]*

Vulgar, ignorant man!

MASHA

Some lucky people don't even notice whether it's winter or
summer. I think that if I were in Moscow, I wouldn't care
about the weather.

VERSHININ

A few days ago I was reading the prison diary of a French
minister. He'd been jailed on account of the Panama
scandal. With what joy, what delight, he writes of the birds
he can see through the prison windows, which he'd never
noticed when he was a minister. Now he's free again, he
notices birds no more than he did before. When you go to
live in Moscow you'll not notice it, either. There can be no
happiness for us, it's just wishful thinking.

TUZENBACH *[Picks up cardboard box]*

Where are the pastries?

IRINA

Soleni has eaten them.

TUZENBACH

All of them?

ANFISA *[Serving tea]*

There's a letter for you, sir.

VERSHININ

For me? *[Takes the letter]* From my daughter. *[Reads]* Yes, of
course ... I have to go. Sorry, Masha. I shan't have any tea.
[Stands up, agitated] Same old story ...

MASHA

What is it? If it's not a secret?

VERSHININ *[Quietly]*

My wife has poisoned herself again. I must go. I'll slip out
quietly. It's all terribly unpleasant. *[Kisses MASHA'S hand]*
My dear, my splendid, good woman ... I'll go this way ...
[Exits.]

ANFISA

Where's he gone? I've brought his tea ... What a man.

MASHA *[Angrily]*

Be quiet! Stop fussing, I can't get a moment's peace ...
[Goes to the table with her cup] I'm tired of you, silly old
woman!

ANFISA

My dear! Why so angry!

ANDREI'S VOICE *[offstage]*

Anfisa!

ANFISA *[Mocking]*

Anfisa! He just sits there and ... *[Exits.]*

MASHA *[In the dining-room, by the table angrily]*
Let me sit down! *[Disturbs the cards on the table]* Cards every-where. Drink your tea.

IRINA
You're in a foul mood, Masha.

MASHA
Well if I am, then don't talk to me. Don't come near me!

CHEBUTIKIN *[laughing]*
Don't go near her, don't go near her ...

MASHA
You're sixty and you're like a little boy, always up to some damned nonsense.

NATASHA *[Sighs]*
Dear Masha, why use such expressions? With your good looks you could be simply enchanting in good society, if it wasn't for your language. – Je vous prie, pardonnez moi, Marie, mais vous avez des manières un peu grossières ...

TUZENBACH *[Trying not to laugh]*
Give me ... give me ... some cognac ...

NATASHA
Il parait, que mon Bobik déjà ne dort pas, – he's awake. He's not well to-day. I'll go to him, excuse me ...

[Exits.]

Tool No. 8: Adjusting Space

Space is really the odd one out. It's not, after all, something you actually do with your own body; it's something around you which you use, or decide not to use. What's important is to understand how you move within space when other people are nearby – how much, or how little, physical space you claim compared to your immediate neighbour. This is your personal space. Imagine it as a flexible invisible bubble: people sense when they have pressed up against your bubble, and you know when you've encroached on someone else's. People claim space through their bodily size and movement, and through their attitude. So to understand space in relation to bodies, you need to be familiar with the other four characteristics of movement – tension, height, openness, and eye contact. All four variables allow you to claim or abandon the space which another person might want.

In the animal world, things tend to be pretty straightforward. (I like the old joke. Q. Where does a crocodile sleep? A. Exactly where it likes.) The degree of relative threat normally determines claims on space: lions lounge in the open, spread over a large area; sheep at night tend to huddle together.

Humanimals of course have to make things more complicated. Use of space is more often a reflection of a person's sense of status relative to others; as a result we engage in daily tussles for space at the breakfast table, on the road to work, in the office, in bed. It is possible to claim a large space – and so a high status – through formal or informal use of objects; picture the caricature of a pompous managing director with a huge desk covering most of his office, and his meek PA perched behind a tiny desk just outside the office door. Or picture two strangers facing each other on a train, a small shared table between them. The large-space-claimer uses bodily openness, height, a relaxed posture, and confident eye contact to stake their claim. This is backed up with assertive use of props – his bag takes up the seat beside him, his can of drink is placed at a point more than halfway across the small shared table, and when he occasionally coughs into his hand he does so with his head up. The small-space-claimer uses small and restricted body movement; his bag stays on his knee, and his drink stays firmly on his 'side' of the table. When he sneezes he does so into his own small space, turning his head down and towards the window. These two characters are basically happy with their respective claims on space. Where things get more interesting is when two people disagree on allocation of space, or when circumstances demand that the 'rules' be suspended.

The first time I ask a new group of students to form a circle, I'm always left with enough space either side of me for at least one, possibly two people. This is the space allocated to me out of respect, or out of shyness. By week two the space between each of us is the same.

Famous people are often allocated a large space, whether they like it or not. A friend described finding a famous composer marooned alone in the middle of a room at a party, complaining distressedly that 'no-one is talking to me!'. Years ago at an awards ceremony in London I was getting ready in my shared dressing room when we were visited by singer Freddie Mercury. He had two 'minders' with him, but there may as well have been ten: the space we allocated to this shy icon seemed to push the rest of us right up against the walls.

Next time you're in a lift with other people, take a few moments to observe the way people claim space around them. Interesting things happen in lifts, where available space is small and unalterable. You don't know, as you wait for the lift doors to open, who will already be in there, or how many people will be inside. You don't know those people's sense of status which will determine their 'claim' on the limited space available. You don't know whether the people already in there are strangers or acquaintances. When the doors open, you have to react instantly, claiming space according to who is already there; most people therefore claim a small space, at least to begin with. People who claim a large space can seem quite rude very quickly, simply by 'invading' the unspoken neutral space allocated by others in the lift. In a crowded lift you would need the hide of a rhinoceros to demand a large space.

People react unconsciously to other people's invisible 'bubbles', as if evading the pressing skin of the other person's space. The head and the body of the lower-status person will be turned slightly away from the power-holder. People's sense of awareness of the 'size' of another person's space – their 'bubble' – can be read partly through the direction they choose to face. When there's no available space – on a crowded London tube train, for example – passengers sardined together into a carriage tend nevertheless to face in different directions, so that the 'challenge' of eye contact is kept to a minimum.

It's different, though, with friends; they are generally happy to share space. Sometimes people who are not friends remain insensitive to other people's demands on space; such 'space invaders' can cause much discomfort to others. This can be due to personality, but also to culture. This was amusingly explored in a TV commercial for a UK bank recently, when an Englishman was shown recoiling from the 'up close' behaviour of locals in Mexico. Once I was mistaken for a local in Spain by an English couple in a bar: when I sat a good six feet away from them, the woman muttered darkly that they were being 'encroached upon'.

Acting tips

An awareness of issues to do with the use of space between people is potentially invaluable for an actor who wants to replicate naturalistic human behaviour. This is one area in which you can dare to trust your instincts moment-by-moment. Unless lighting or camera angles dictate otherwise, your use of space between you and your fellow actors ought at least subtly to change from performance to performance. Moving within space is something we do in reaction, as well as when taking action; so if you really are psychologically 'tuned in' to your fellow actors, there will be a fluid and changing use of space in response to your interaction with them. Once again, muscular tension brought on by a mental state of unreadiness is the most inhibiting factor in relation to the effective use of space onstage; you have to be able to focus on, and listen hard to, your fellow actors before your reactions can be genuine and spontaneous. Get rid of your script as early as possible in rehearsal. Practise listening.

One interesting rehearsal technique requires the actors in a scene to make choices about use of the space between them. Briefly, you run a scene and at any moment you have to do one of three things: keep still; move closer to another actor; or move away from another actor. At the rehearsal stage this activity is intended to promote discovery, to allow each actor to externalise his feelings towards other characters; movement should therefore be decisive and significant. As rehearsals progress, any such movement may become more subtle or may even disappear: a character may be left with a psychological desire to move away from another character, but may be inhibited from doing so by some important factor such as a desire to save face, or to hide his real feelings. What remains, then, is a hidden and appropriate sense of tension.

Exercises: Solo

1) Next time you find yourself in a confined space with others – on a train, for example, or in a lift – try to visualise the proportions of your personal space 'bubble'. Then visualise it as being much bigger. Allow yourself some bodily movement which expresses the sense that you have a larger personal space. Maintain this for some time and see how it affects your own feelings. Note also whether other people alter their behaviour towards you.

2) Choose a modern naturalistic monologue you're comfortable with and know well. Select one in which there is another character in the scene, even though your audience cannot see them. Restage the monologue, using your full knowledge of space issues in relation to other people.

Exercises: Partnered

1) Think of a situation in which two strangers might meet. Using a scale of one to ten, choose a level of confidence for

each of you: low, medium, or high. Create a 'back story' to support your behaviour. Enter the set situation when you're ready, and behave as truthfully as you can within the situation. As an actor, concentrate on staying aware of your use of space during the scene. Run the scene again – but this time the characters are friends.

2) People sometimes use objects to help them claim space in relation to others. Select some small items for possible use; the ones you used in the Openness exercises will do. Prepare a scene which requires that there should be a table between characters. During the scene, make 'strategic' use of your items to help you either to claim more space, or to withdraw into a smaller space.

3) Think of a social situation in which two people might meet. Plan a moment in your scene at which something big changes the relative status between the two characters – a decision, perhaps, or a revelation. Explore during the scene how each character's claim on space alters before, during and after the 'moment'. Try running the scene as (a) strangers; (b) friends; (c) lovers.

4) Run a scene in a lift in which both characters are comfortable with the relative space between them. Re-run the scene with one of the characters showing insensitivity towards the other character's spatial claim. If you have more than two actors, add additional characters to explore how new arrivals complicate things.

Example: Natasha from *Three Sisters*

Read and rehearse this scene below, again from Act Two. This is a difficult scene for Natasha. Guests are still in her house, and her husband is here too. Yet she seems to have made arrangements with her lover Protopopov for him to call and take her out. As she juggles these matters, and then confronts Irina with her decision to move her into Olga's room, Natasha's use of space could well suggest her state of mind:

[*NATASHA enters with a candle; she looks in through one door, then through another, and goes past the door leading to her husband's room.*]

NATASHA

There's Andrei. Let him go on reading. Sorry, Vassili Vassilevitch, I didn't know you were here; I'm not dressed.

SOLENI

It's all the same to me. Goodnight! [*Exit.*]

NATASHA

You're so tired, my poor dear girl! [*Kisses IRINA*] If you only went to bed earlier.

IRINA

Is Bobik asleep?

NATASHA

Yes, but he's restless. By the way, dear, I wanted to tell you, but either you were out, or I was busy ... I think Bobik's nursery is cold and damp. And your room would be so right for the child. My dear, do move over to Olga's for a bit!

IRINA [*Not understanding*]
Where?

[*The bells of a troika are heard as it drives up to the house.*]

NATASHA

You and Olga can share a room, for the time being, and Bobik can have yours. He's such a darling; to-day I said to him, 'Bobik, you're mine! Mine!' And he looked at me with his dear little eyes. [*A bell rings*] It must be Olga. She's very late. [*The maid enters and whispers to NATASHA*] Protopopov? What an odd man. Protopopov's come and wants me to go for a ride with him in his troika. *[Laughs]* How funny men are ... *[A bell rings]* Somebody's at the door. I suppose I could pop out for a quick ride ... *[To the maid]* Say I shan't be long. *[Bell rings]* The bell again, it must be Olga.

[Exits.]

section 4: **the voice**

Voice is quite simply the sound you make. Speech is the use of lips and tongue to shape, and to control, that sound into words. In this Section we're concerned mainly with voice, and how it supports the meaning of speech.

Actors use their voices to ensure effective communication to an audience, and to express things which may be hidden 'behind' the spoken words in a script.

We will consider four new Tools which expand your range as an expressive performer. Tool Number 9 – Adjusting Loudness – takes a common-sense look at one of the key elements of effective onstage performance. Tool Number 10 – Adjusting Inflection – explores how changes in the musical notes in your voice can carry emotion, and can radically alter the meaning of words or phrases. Tool Number 11 – Adjusting Note – examines how a character's 'true root note' can alter audience perceptions, and develops the link between note and inflection. Tool Number 12 – Adjusting Tone – assesses how the 'hardness' or 'softness' of a character's tone of voice can carry important associations.

As before, we'll look first at what each term means; we'll look behind the term to see what knowledge is required to be able to change each variable; we'll consider the psychological reasons why the relevant characteristic will vary from person to person; and I'll end with some suggested exercises to help you improve your control over each vocal characteristic.

Just as two people's physical behaviour can be very different, so too can there be huge variations in two people's vocal behaviour. Just as parts of your own body language may be 'wrong' for a character you're playing, so too can aspects of your own vocal behaviour be inappropriate. It's important that you develop an understanding of the characteristics of your own voice and speech, so that you can use that knowledge in practice as an actor.

What then are the key 'variables' in voice? The word **LINT** captures the four key changeables: **L**oudness, **I**nflection, **N**ote, and **T**one.

Ideally you should use a dictaphone to help you work through the vocal sections of this book. Record and replay your efforts as often as possible: you should get used to hearing even the subtlest differences in your own voice. With practice and a good 'ear' you will be amazed at how vocally versatile you can become.

Tool No. 9: Adjusting Loudness

Your own natural speaking voice will be loud, quiet, or somewhere in between. As an actor you need to develop the control and sensitivity required to vary volume. The basic reason is obvious: the audience member sitting high up in a theatre's 'gods' must be able to hear all the words spoken by you, every bit as clearly as the person sat in the front row of the stalls.

In a moment we'll look at the techniques of volume control. First, though, let's put the issue of vocal volume into context in everyday life. Vocal volume in the real world can reveal important psychological things about a person. Let's start with the clichés: a confident person is always loud; a shy person is always quiet. Like most clichés, there's a lot of truth in this. Confidence – real, unforced confidence – may well be expressed in part through a loud, clear voice. The speaker is secure in his opinions and is happy for anyone to hear them. A shy person lacks confidence in their ability to communicate well. They may doubt the appropriateness of their own opinion. In an effort to limit damage to their confidence, they will tend to keep their voice at a quiet level.

So far so obvious. But, as with physical communication, things get rather more interesting when the speaker tries to disguise their feelings. Someone who normally thinks of themselves as being shy, may find themselves in a situation where they must seem confident: making a speech at a wedding, for example. So they do their best to be vocally louder. If they're sufficiently in control, then they do a good job of disguising their shyness, and manage to sound confident. If the stress of the situation takes over, they may actually speak far too loudly. Consider also the super-confident person who is attracted to a shy person at a party. The former responds to the need to avoid bulldozing the latter by adopting a quieter, more intimate vocal level.

How, then, do you gain control over vocal volume? As with so many other things, you learn the theory, you explore the processes, and you practise, practise, practise. And as with so many other things in acting, the basis of good vocal volume control is relaxation – the ability to relax physically and mentally.

Here in brief is the process which leads to you making a sound:

- You take a breath.
- You breathe out.
- As you breathe out, some of the air passes over the vocal cords in your throat.
- You allow the air to vibrate the vocal cords.
- The sound you produce is your voice.

So far, so straightforward. So what do actors do to give them greater control over vocal volume?

Mainly, they learn to relax under pressure. A relaxed body is a body freed of muscular tension. It's no coincidence that vocal exercises are often done with the student laid flat on the floor: this position requires virtually no muscle tension.

There are real benefits to being able to stay physically relaxed during performance. You can take a bigger breath. You have greater control over the outward flow of breath. Resonance, which helps to amplify your voice, will be enhanced. What, then, is resonance?

Resonance occurs when sound is amplified through effective use of resonators. What are resonators? Resonators are spaces: chambers of varying size, dotted about your upper body. Your mouth is a resonator; so is your nose; so is your throat; so are your lungs. So, too, are your sinuses – the tiny chambers which are peppered around your skull. Each of these resonators has the potential to help amplify your voice. Picture two guitars: one is a solid-bodied electric guitar, the other is a hollow-bodied acoustic guitar. If you strum the strings on the electric guitar, without plugging it into an amplifier, you might well struggle to hear the resulting sound from across a room. If you do the same thing to the acoustic guitar, the sound resonates in the hollow body of the guitar, amplifying the sound hugely. The hollow body of the guitar is the guitar's resonator.

How can we be sure that it is the empty space which is respons-ible for amplifying the guitar's sound? If you fill the hollow body of the guitar with some sort of material – cotton-wool, say, or cloth – the reduction in the availability of empty space in the hol-low body causes a massive reduction in resonance, which in turn leads to a significant reduction in volume. It's the same with the human body. If you're very tense, you start to restrict and reduce your resonators; so you get less amplification through resonance. If you have a bad cold, and your nose and sinuses are blocked, you will notice a marked reduction in volume. This deadening effect results from the blocked resonators being inactive.

There's already a great deal of help and advice available to support the actor who wants to improve his vocal projection (see Further Reading), so, with apologies, I'm going to move on.

Acting tips
There's not too much benefit in analysing the psychology behind levels of vocal volume, for the simple reason that an actor

onstage must clearly maintain a significant level of volume whatever his character's given circumstances. The need to be audible must override any notions of 'realism'; this is a simple golden rule, a 'given'. An audience may sometimes forgive less-than-brilliant acting, but if you speak too quietly and deny them access to the story, they'll not forgive that.

In the recorded media, if the director can't hear all of your words, you'll be stopped and there will be a retake. The sound recordist will try to take account of your vocal volume, but you may be asked speak up, or even reduce your vocal volume. This is harder than it sounds if you're acting an emotional scene. Always remember, though, that you're working in a commercial environment – someone in the hierarchy has deemed that the words matter. Just do your best; it's unlikely that people will notice your private awkwardness.

Exercises: Solo

Here is a list of exercises to do in sequence, to help you to achieve greater vocal volume. Make sure that your body is in a relaxed position before you start each exercise.

1) Lie on the floor, face up, and relax your body fully. Breathe regularly through your nose, imagining, as you breathe in, that your navel is being drawn towards the ceiling. (This helps to ensure that your breathing makes use of your diaphragm muscle, which is located just above your navel.) Let your teeth be parted but keep your lips together. As you breathe out, allow the air to pass over your vocal cords, so that you make a sound. Don't try to form any words, just make a simple sound: you are gently activating the vocal cords, and amplifying the sound through your natural resonators. The sound you make, a gentle 'mmmm' sound, should be roughly on the same note, but, because you're not singing, the note will glide downwards a little as you run out of breath. You should feel a slight tickling sensation on your lips.

2) This is a continuation of the first exercise. This time, as you breathe out, after three seconds let your jaw drop so that your mouth falls open: visualise the sound as being released from confinement. The sound you make will be a gentle 'mmmaaah'. You'll notice, with some practice, that, with relatively little effort from you, and without any attempt to shout, your voice is surprisingly loud. Check for tension; your mouth and throat are large resonators which will work more effectively as such if they are open and relaxed. Yawn, noticing the open position of the throat and the back of your mouth. Aim for a relaxed version of this position when you're breathing out. Practise this exercise daily; you'll become familiar with the power of resonance, and you will also get used to being relaxed when you create sound.

3) Do as you did before in 2), but also practise controlling the flow of breath more carefully. Count in your head how many seconds you take to breathe in, then to breathe out. In normal speech, we tend to take a very short breath in, and then we control the outward flow of air over a period of a few seconds. Be aware that when you work on verse or classical texts, you can't always take a breath when you feel like it; you may need to wait until the end of a long line. Over time, train yourself to be able to take a big breath, which you release in a controlled way, through a relaxed body, making good use of your resonators.

4) Repeat the exercises above, but do them standing up. Stand with your feet slightly apart, your weight evenly balanced, arms by your sides. You need few muscles to stay in this position – mainly just the muscles around your ankles and your knees. Keep everything else as relaxed as possible. The challenge is to maintain strong amplification through use of your resonators, even though some muscles need to be tensed. Note just how few muscle groups are required to stand like this. Later, when you're in a social situation, notice how many more muscles you use – frowning, tensing the jaw, pressing thumb against fingers, clawing feet, tilting neck at an

angle, placing weight mainly on one hip; these are some of the common areas of added tension. As an actor you need to develop an awareness of which muscles are tense, so that you can relax those which are tensed unnecessarily.

Tool No. 10: Adjusting Inflection

Inflection describes the way in which we move through different notes when using our voices.

As you'll see, we do tend to think of inflection as a characteristic of speech, rather than of voice. But I'm going to cheat and introduce it here in the section on Voice, not just because you can actually alter inflection without using language, but because we often do. And when we do, vocal inflection is often inextricably linked to our spontaneous emotions. A yawn, for example, requires you to make a simple non-speech sound, which typically slides from a higher note to a lower one. And a yawn can carry considerable meaning in terms of a person's attitude and state of mind: try a few pretend yawns now, and widen the range of notes which you pass through as you yawn. Think also of the 'mmm' sound we make when something tastes good: the voice slides, without use of words, from one note to another. The vocal sound which accompanies any intense sensual or psychological experience – pain, laughter, pleasure – each can easily be voiced using a non-speech-based change in inflection.

To consider how we alter inflection, it's probably easiest to think, initially, about singing: a song with only one note would be extremely dull, so the singer varies the notes during the song. Think of the old rhyming song 'Three Blind Mice'. It begins with three simple notes: a high note for 'three', a lower note for 'blind', and a lower note still for 'mice'. Fast-forward now to the section which runs, 'They all run after the farmer's wife'. Sing it. (If you're reading this on a train, hum it. If you're reading this on a train, and you want more space around you, sing it.) This time, the melody uses four notes. The singer follows a pattern which, during that particular line, uses most of those notes more than once. If the singer can read music, he may use a score, which will guide him in knowing when a note is repeated. For a singer, a musical score is in essence a guide to inflection: it tells the singer whether the next note to be sung is higher, lower, or the same as the previous note.

In speech, vocal inflection helps the listener to follow meaning. At some point in your life you'll have come across the person who speaks in a monotonous voice, meaning they speak virtually on a single note. Have a go now at speaking on a single note. (This should get you even more space on the train.)

Not only would this be boring to listen to, it would be very difficult for the listener to pick out which parts of the spoken sentence are most important. So the speaker – even, if you listen carefully, the boring speaker – takes the trouble to vary the notes.

Take the last three words from that sentence: 'vary the notes'. Good advice, that. Keep your voice interesting by varying the notes.

Now look at that last sentence – the one you've just read which begins, 'Keep your voice...'. Imagine you're about to make a speech, and this sentence is the first line of your speech. Decide for yourself which are the most important words in the sentence (pick a maximum of four). Here is the sentence again, in isolation:

- Keep your voice interesting by varying the notes.

One interpretation would give the following capitalized words the most importance:

- KEEP your voice INTERESTING by VARYING the NOTES.

Read the sentence out loud, stressing the words which are in capitals. In order to do this, you will have to vary the notes. (The only other choice you have is to make the words in capitals louder, which sounds odd. Try it.) Most likely, you will have used a slightly higher note for the words in capitals. As I said earlier, it's a good idea to have a dictaphone with you when you're doing exercises like this. If you have one, use it now, repeating the sentence and accentuating the words which need stressing. Play it back, and listen for the (possibly subtle) changes in use of note.

Listening to a speaker is not, of course, the same as listening to a singer. A singer follows notes which a composer has previously scored; even the duration for which the singer should hold a note will be predetermined. The speaker, however, is providing a spontaneous score, and the resulting score reveals things about the speaker's feelings and attitudes.

There is another, fairly obvious way in which the inflection of a speaker differs from the inflection of a singer. The singer has a fixed range of notes to choose from. If the singer fails to reach a note cleanly, the listener notices (and probably winces). The speaker has a range of notes in his repertoire limited only by his vocal range. There's no such thing as being 'off key' for a speaker: pretty well anything goes, as long as the chosen inflection supports the speaker's meaning.

Another difference: the speaker habitually slides between notes, whereas the singer generally does not. Go back to the line from 'Three Blind Mice' which runs: 'They all run after the farmer's wife'. Sing the line again. Now sing it a second time, but this time allow yourself to slide from one note to another (you'll probably sound drunk!). Take it a little further. Start to think of the sentence as being a spoken sentence: you're telling the story to a child, and the child asks: 'So what happens to the mice next?' You reply, 'They all run after the farmer's wife.' When you say the line, keep in your mind the 'sung' version. Speak the line, keeping approximately to the notes in the 'sung' version, but try to make the sentence work as a genuine, spoken reply to the child's question. When you do this, you are consciously using vocal inflection.

Once you become aware of vocal inflection in speech, you can start to use inflection consciously. Actors need to be conscious of, and able to control, inflection. Much of the time, an actor's awareness of his use of inflection simply helps him to avoid sounding dull. But some jobs require an actor to be extremely competent in controlling vocal inflection. Voice-over work for commercials relies on the actor being fully vocally responsive to the needs of the director. A director working with a voice-over artist will often ask the actor to alter his emphasis on a particular word or phrase; this usually means he wants a different vocal inflection.

It's always worth remembering that inflection is a characteristic of voice as well as of speech. In real life, vocal inflection is something to which listeners respond with great sensitivity. Say the phrase out loud, 'that's interesting'. Sound as if you mean it, as if you've just read something which impresses you. You'll probably find that you've spoken the line with a vocal inflection which rises significantly at some point during the phrase. Now say the phrase again, but this time, artificially reduce the range of your vocal inflection. The statement will now sound less sincere, tinged with irony or sarcasm. The words are the same; the vocal inflection, when altered, changes the message.

The use of a wide range of notes generally suggests enthusiasm and sincerity – though too much variety in notes can tip you over into sounding insincere. Using a narrow range of notes, or under-inflecting, suggests a lack of enthusiasm or cynicism. Among some people, especially teenagers, it can be considered 'uncool' to be enthusiastic about things in general. The inflection pattern among such groups can become limited to a narrow range of notes, partly in reaction to authority figures whose wider range of vocal inflection expresses enthusiasm. It's worth noting that if you under-inflect and combine this with an apparently interested facial expression, the mixed message can seem very sarcastic indeed.

Acting tips

Listen to vocal inflection around you, and secretly mimic it. You're copying the pattern of notes, not the words, so you can get away with humming the inflections under your breath. 'Real' conversations have a huge variety of inflection range. Most people are untrained in voice-use, so they're fairly unaware of their inflection pattern. Regional accent is relevant here: some accents have very distinct vocal inflection patterns. Indeed, with some accents you can often identify the accent just from the vocal inflection pattern without hearing any actual speech (the Brummy or Birmingham accent in the United Kingdom is a good example).

Mimic also broadcasters – newsreaders, radio presenters, journalists. Journalists who deliver reports 'from the field' often have peculiar inflection patterns which seem to have almost random stresses, but are accepted as part of the field reporter's 'voice'. The man who reads the football results on television on Saturdays famously uses vocal inflection which is predictable: you know whether it's a home win, a draw, or an away win halfway through his announcement. Try the following score in different ways:

Liverpool	1	Arsenal	1	
Chelsea	2	Southampton	1	
Manchester United	0	Everton	5	(Well – you never know.)

Most radio DJs use a very wide range of notes indeed. They're trying to sound energised, enthusiastic, interesting.

Newsreaders use a wider or narrower range of notes depending on the news item. Most news is delivered with a wide range of notes, to help clarify meaning; but the death of a well-loved celebrity is always delivered with a more limited inflection. Try reading a selection of pieces from a newspaper with this in mind.

Exercises: Solo

1) Refer back to the exercises in the 'Loudness' section. This time, as you breathe out, vary your vocal inflection, letting your voice slide upwards and then down again. Increase the frequency of variation, and use a wider range of notes each time (but avoid going into a falsetto voice). You'll probably notice, as you do this, that different resonators come into play, depending on the note you reach. On a high note you can feel vibration in your nose and forehead; on a low note you can feel it in your throat and chest.

2) Similar to 1), but using your imagination as a stimulus. First, let yourself release a plain, monotonous sound. Now concentrate on an image of, and on the memory of the taste of, your favourite food. Let yourself release a vocal sound again, but this time allow your feelings towards the imagined stimulus (the food) to alter the inflection. Try it with other imagined stimuli: unpleasant as well as pleasant images, intensely pleasurable memories as well as unpleasant ones.

3) Pick a nursery rhyme. Sing it. Sing it again and again, slowly converting the singing into speech by 'sliding' between notes. You'll probably find that you need to reduce the pitch of the highest notes in order to stop the piece sounding too 'sung'. Try to convert it from a sung rhyme to a spoken phrase without sacrificing all of the original tune, and try to allow some sort of spoken meaning to come through. Try to make the inflection pattern 'make sense'.

Exercises: Partnered

1) Have a conversation with your partner – without using any words. Instead, have an idea in your head of what the words would be, but just use voice; varying the inflection will help your partner to understand your meaning. Try to avoid adding mimed gestures (if you find you're miming too much, do the exercise with your eyes shut).

2) Refer back to the beginning of the section on Inflection. Select a range of non-language vocal sounds which people often use to express spontaneous feelings and attitudes: yawning, laughter, responses to physical pain or pleasure, responses to mental moods of happiness or sadness. Working with your partner, devise a short scene in which an interaction takes place using only sounds and actions (i.e. don't use words at all).

Tool No. 11: Adjusting Note

Every individual has a note which I'm calling the 'true root note' for their voice. By this I mean that you have a natural vocal note which you make when you're fully relaxed, for example when you vocalise a yawn in private. You've probably already demonstrated your own true root note: this was the spontaneous vocal sound you made while completely relaxed in the first solo exercise in the 'Loudness' section.

People do of course have different root notes. Partly this is physiological; men tend to have larger and less tightened vocal cords, and larger resonators, so they tend to have a lower root note which amplifies well. Women tend to have shorter and tighter vocal cords, which creates a higher root note; and the resonators which accompany and amplify that higher note tend to be smaller.

In adulthood, some people develop a voice which is rooted at a pitch which is different from their true root note. The reason for developing a 'public root note' – a higher or lower root note which a person uses in public, and which becomes, by habit, the core of their 'new' voice – is usually psychological. Over a period of years people can become socialised into behaving in ways that other people expect. For girls and women, a soft-toned voice delivered on a fairly high note can seem appealing to men, by dint of it sounding unthreatening: the caricature example of this has to be Marilyn Monroe. A girl who has a fairly low true root note may be teased for having a 'manly' voice. A higher true root note in a man is often considered inappropriate; footballer David Beckham draws critical comment for having a voice which uses a lot of higher notes.

It's hardly surprising then that girls and women can lose contact with their lower true root note, and develop instead a higher public root note. Men can adopt a voice which is centred at a note lower than their true root note in order to sound 'manly'. Men living within a gay culture can develop, over time, a public root note which is higher than their true root note.

This loss of contact with your true root note can become a problem if you're an actor. Partly, this has to do with vocal projection. In theatre, a voice which uses a lot of high notes gains only limited support from resonators: the voice doesn't carry so well. Also, a voice which has developed away from its owner's true root note is not going to be as 'in contact' with that person's emotions. So it's worth reflecting on whether this has happened to you; and if it has, it's worth making the effort to rediscover your true root note. This is not as hard as it sounds, but it will take time. You'll need to do voice exercises regularly, and you'll need to monitor your voice use in everyday conversation. The first two solo exercises in the 'Loudness' section should be repeated daily; monitor your progress using a dictaphone. Do the exercises in the 'Inflection' section, too; these will help you to reach any specific vocal note.

We're going to focus now on the way in which a combination of vocalised notes can alter the meaning of a spoken phrase. We've had a first look at this in the previous Section; we're now going to explore in more detail the relationship between note and inflection.

For this Section, you'll need to be familiar with the 'doh ray mee' musical scale (remember *The Sound of Music*?). This musical scale simply places notes in order to form an octave (the series of eight notes which musicians and singers use as part of musical notation). You don't need to be able to read music.

Hum out loud the first three notes – doh, ray, me. Make sure that you're relaxed, so that your starting note is close to your true root note. Hum the three notes a few times. Now hum them in the order, me, doh, ray. Practise it a couple of times so that you can be sure you've hit the right notes. Now take the word 'hello'. Sing the word 'hello', keeping the tune in the order which you've just been practising: me, doh, ray. (You'll probably sound like a medieval monk.) Now repeat the word, but alter it so that you are sliding between the three notes. Practise this, imagining that you're greeting somebody. You're now using your conscious awareness of how notes form an inflection pattern within speech.

Take it a little further now. Go through the octave again, starting at doh, and stop when you get to tee. Work out and remember the simple sequence tee, doh, ray. Once again using the word 'hello', transform this into a realistic spoken greeting. Practise it.

Think, now, about the difference between the two ways in which you spoke the word 'hello'. Technically, in the second version you started on a higher note. Ask yourself how the change of note might alter the meaning behind the greeting. Here's one interpretation. The first time you say hello, you're not surprised to see the person, but you suspect that they might have been up to something. Your objective is: 'I want to know what you've been up to.' The second time you say hello, you're greeting someone you haven't seen for a long time, and you're pleased to see them. You objective is: 'I want you to stay and chat.'

Let's try a simple third version. This time, keep entirely on the note 'doh' throughout the word 'hello': in other words, say the word on low monotone. How does this sound? What could the meaning be behind this delivery of the greeting? Perhaps the person you're speaking to is someone you've been hiding from because they irritate you, and they've just found you. Your objective might be: 'I want you to go away'.

One more to try. Go back to the first time you said 'hello'. You used the three notes in the order me, doh, ray. Hum 'doh' again. Now sing your way up the octave, so that you reach the next 'doh' up (an octave above the previous one). Find the three notes 'me, doh, ray' within this higher octave. Convert this again into a greeting using the word 'hello'. How has the meaning changed? One interpretation is that, although you are still suspicious of the person, you really didn't expect to see them. Your objective is still: 'I want to know what you've been up to;' but now you might also be wondering, 'How on earth did they know I would be here?'

Acting tip

I'm not advocating that you should deconstruct a naturalistic script in this way; it's a tortuous process at the best of times, and you'll be guaranteed to lose some spontaneity if everything is rigidly pre-planned. The point of the exercises is to help you see that the choice of note, and the pattern of inflection, do greatly matter to an audience: a listener will pick up on the most acute of subtleties if the actor is aware of what he is doing. When you're playing the sort of character who is adept at controlling his face and body to hide his real feelings – a high-status public figure, for example – then vocal note and inflection become crucial to effective communication, both to your audience and to your fellow actors.

Exercises: Solo

1) Start experimenting with changing your own root note. Begin by copying the voices of both men and women on television; then try setting a noticeably different root note when you're briefly with strangers, and see if they ever react differently to you. Try out a subtler change of root note when you're with friends, and see if there's any difference in the way they treat you.

2) Select a monologue from a naturalistic play. Record a good sight-reading of the speech on your dictaphone, using a slow pace. Listen to the recording, paying close attention to the choices of note and inflection. Replay the speech, and, as the recording plays, speak the speech out loud again, making very different choices of root note and inflection. Record the second, different version of the speech as closely as you can from memory. Listen to both; reflect on how different 'meanings' were created by the two different versions of the speech.

Exercises: Partnered

1) Think of an everyday situation in which two people might meet and chat casually. Begin an improvised conversation. Become aware of the root notes and inflection pattern you're using during the conversation: try if you can to create an imaginary 'retrospective score' in your head as you 'hear' the notes and inflection you're using.

2) Repeat the exercise. This time, place one hand in front of you, with your forefinger pointing away from you. Each time you speak, let your forefinger rise or fall in response to the pattern of your vocal inflection (if you're speaking on a monotone, your finger will of course be still). Ask your partner to speak very slowly, and use your hand to retrospectively 'score' their inflection pattern in the air. The lower the root note, the lower your finger is in the air.

3) Repeat the first exercise again. At random points, repeat any phrase of several words, with precisely the same choice of notes and inflection that you've just used spontaneously.

4) Below is the script for a situation in which two people might meet and chat casually. Make two copies for each actor. On each copy, mark definite and bold choices of note and inflection pattern that differ from those in the other script. Run each version. Discuss with your partner how the different choices of note and inflection affect the way your partner reacts to you.

A: Hello.

B: Hello.

A: Cold isn't it?

B: It is.

A: Have we met before?

B: Have we? I don't know.

A: I think we have.

B: When?

A: I don't know.

B: No.

Tool No. 12: Adjusting Tone

Tone is a term which is used to describe the degree of 'hardness' or 'softness' in the quality of a person's voice. It's difficult to describe and to identify tonal quality, but it can have a very strong impact on the listener.

There are similarities between the tone of a voice, and the tone settings on a hi-fi audio system. Many audio systems have controls which allow you to increase or reduce the strength of the bass, and the strength of the treble qualities in music. More sophisticated systems allow you to alter the tone of a piece of music in very subtle ways, through the use of a graphic equaliser. The bass, treble and middle frequencies can be balanced to levels which suit each individual listener. When you turn up the frequency control on, say, the bass section of an audio system, you are in effect increasing the degree of bass resonance, and not just turning up the bass volume. If you already have the music turned up loud on a really powerful system, you can find that the bass notes in a piece of music vibrate so strongly through the speakers that you can feel vibration in your own body.

It's important to remember that like musical tone, vocal tone is a quality which can be altered when sound is pitched and held on a single note. Any note you can sing comfortably can be altered to have a harder, or a softer, tone.

Let's stick with the idea of vocal tone being 'hard' or 'soft'. What are the judgements that we, as listeners, attach to voices with hard or soft tonal qualities? A soft-toned voice tends to lend a speaker the sense of being gentle, thoughtful, relaxed. Caricature examples might be a child-counsellor, or a late-night DJ. A hard-toned voice can make a speaker seem energised, spontaneous, tense. Caricature examples might be a market trader, or a presenter on a youth TV channel.

As a general rule, a regional accent which is associated with a city tends to have a harsher tone than a regional accent which is associated with a country area. People use their breath, tension, and resonance in slightly different ways. People from rural Ireland, for example, tend to release a fairly smooth and continuous flow of air when speaking, which is more conducive to allowing vocal resonance. Natives of Belfast, however, tend to interrupt the flow of air quite a lot, which adds physical tension to the throat and so reduces resonance. They do this by use of what is known as a glottal stop. When considering vocal tone, it's worth clarifying precisely what a glottal stop is.

A glottal stop occurs when the back of the throat is momentarily tensed during speech, halting the flow of air. Try this. Say out loud the word 'automatic', with a strong Cockney accent: it comes out as 'au'o'ma'ic', with at least three glottal stops within that single word. Do it again. This time trap your delivery of the word after the first bit, so that you say only 'au'. Note the position of your throat: it's tensed and closed; no air can get through.

Think back now to the section on 'Loudness', where we looked at resonance. Resonators work best when air is allowed to flow freely and the muscles around the resonators are relaxed. Vocal tone – whether a person's voice sounds hard or soft in tone – depends most of all on these two factors: flow of air, and bodily tension.

So what can you do to alter the tone of your own voice? It's not easy to alter tone in any significant way. Vocal tone is like regional accent, in that it's something which you've developed throughout your life and which has become instinctive. If you want to vary tone, you'll need to gain full control over both the flow of air when you're breathing out, and the degree to which you are physically relaxed. It helps also to develop a sense of 'placement of the voice', visualising your voice as being 'centred' at a particular point along the route of the flow of air. If you're trying to achieve a soft vocal tone, it can be helpful to visualise the voice as having been placed in the centre of your chest: keep as many muscles as possible relaxed, and focus on feeling the vibration in your chest resonator (think 'late-night DJ'). If you're trying to achieve a hard vocal tone, visualise the voice as having been placed in the throat, or in the mouth (think 'youth TV presenter'). Be careful in theatre, though. 'Placing' the voice in the throat will inevitably create some degree of muscle tension there, and if you're struggling to project your voice, tension can lead to long-term damage. In recorded media such as TV and radio such tension is sustainable as long as you're not having to project your voice.

Acting tip

Your own 'natural' vocal tone will be located somewhere between 'hard' and 'soft'. The more extreme your tone, the greater the need to develop the sensitivity to change it. So listen carefully to the differing vocal tone of ordinary people. Listen also to voice-overs for television commercials; the type of product being marketed will dictate the choice of vocal tone used. Sometimes the same actor can be heard using different tones within different commercials. If you find that you can master the ability to alter tone, you may well become that bit more employable as an actor.

Exercises: Solo

Perform the following solo exercises daily, using your dictaphone to monitor your progress. Bear in mind that the microphone on a typical dictaphone will not capture the subtleties of changes in vocal tone; if you're really serious about wanting to achieve control over vocal tone, invest in better-quality recording equipment.

1) Go back to the first exercise in the 'Loudness' section. Begin by repeating the original exercise. Then, as you breathe out, experiment with subtle variations of tension which will alter your vocal tone. Use visualisation to 'place' your voice at points on a range between the centre of your chest, and your lips. The visualisation is intended as a mental guide only: technically, you will be subtly adding muscular tension to harden the tone, and removing tension to soften the tone.
2) Repeat 1), but this time maintain a relaxed muscular state, and change the note each time you breathe out. Observe how your vocal tone seems to harden each time you choose an increasingly higher note, and to soften when you use

lower notes. Remember that the lower the note, the more you are using chest and neck resonance.

3) Transcribe voice-over 'tag lines' from television and radio commercials. Practise speaking the words using varying degrees of hard and soft tone. Record your work, and listen to the differences.

Exercises: Partnered

1) Find a scene which contains some dialogue between two characters (you could initially use the short dialogue in Partnered exercise 4) in the 'Note' section). Allocate a particular tone to each character – a hard tone for one, a soft tone for the other. Try to make sure that both characters use roughly the same root note. Read it aloud. Swap tones between characters. Discuss with your partner how different qualities of tone suit different characters. Try another duologue.

2) As before, but this time allow your characters to use significantly different root notes, one high, one low – the idea being to use differing levels of resonance. 'Swap' tone. Discuss how different qualities of tone work for the different characters. Try another duologue.

3) As in 1) above, but this time allow your tone to slowly transform during the scene, e.g. from soft to hard. This is one of the transformations which can occur spontaneously in response to emotional state – when the speaker is feeling threatened, for example.

section 5 : **speech**

Voice, then, is the sound that you make. Speech is how you control the sound, to convert it into words. Speech in theatre generally carries much of the important information required by an audience. As such, it is absolutely central to the job of acting.

Actors use speech to communicate important information, not just about the story of the play, but also about the personality of their character.

In this Section you will be introduced to four new Tools to help you become a more sophisticated communicator, and a more versatile actor. Tool Number 13 – Varying the Pace – assesses how speed of speech represents an often-overlooked characteristic of personality, and how varying pace of speech can have important effects. Tool Number 14 – Changing Accent – examines one of the most popular methods of altering character, and offers tips on how to develop expertise in using accents. Tool Number 15 – Focus on Diction – underlines the importance of clear diction for actors; and Tool Number 16 – Employing Specials – walks through some of the most common speech variations, with advice on how they can be achieved.

Once again, we'll look first at what each term means; we'll consider what knowledge is required to be able to change each variable; we'll consider the psychological reasons for variations between people; and I'll end with some suggested speech exercises. As before, use your dictaphone liberally.

Speech has four key variable characteristics: **P**ace, **A**ccent, **D**iction, and what I've called '**S**pecials'. Together they form the mnemonic '**PADS**'. If you put together the variable characteristics of body, voice and speech, you have the mnemonic phrase **THOSE LINT PADS**. Odd though the phrase may be, it works well as an 'aide-memoire' for all the things a transformational character actor can change. If you want to achieve effective transformational character acting, **use those lint pads**.

Tool No. 13: Varying the Pace

Pace describes simply the speed at which speech takes place. As with most personal characteristics, pace of speech is something which we only really notice if there's something irritating about it – something harmful to speech communication. The two obvious extremes are, speech so rapid that the listener is unable to keep up; and speech so slow that it becomes frustrating to listen to.

Different speeds of speech create different perceptions of the speaker. Fast speech can suggest confidence, quick-wittedness, spontaneity, energy. Slow speech can suggest reticence, low intelligence, cautiousness, listlesness. But fast speech can also suggest nervousness; and slow speech can be the sign of a confident person who chooses to dictate the pace of communication.

As we explored earlier, people hide things. The nervous person will often try to seem confident and in control. The naturally enthusiastic person may try to hide their enthusiasm in order to seem 'cool'. Both illusions can be achieved by altering the pace of speech.

It's really valuable for an actor to have an awareness of pace. One of the challenges of acting, especially in a full-length theatre production, is to maintain an audience's attention throughout the 'arc' of the play. A good story will keep them listening, but you, as a key communicator of that story, shoulder much of the responsibility for keeping them really interested. And an awareness of pace of speech is a valuable, and underused, weapon in the fight to remain interesting.

Of course, you shouldn't ever change pace simply in an attempt to remain interesting; pace of speech is a reflection of a person's mental and emotional state, so at any point in a play there will be a pace of speech which is appropriate. Nor should you over-prepare by trawling through your script to plan pace of speech. Understand your character's journey through the play, and then in rehearsal do those crucial things which actors must do – keep focused, stay relaxed, listen – and you'll find that your pace of speech shifts spontaneously in reaction to your character's circumstances. And of course it follows that the speed at which you deliver a line may well alter in response to the performance of your fellow actor.

The best acting performances have an organic quality about them; the actor maintains a psychological and emotional responsiveness, which alters his performance each time. In order to develop the skills needed to 'let go' – in order to achieve confidence in allowing things like your pace of speech to change spontaneously – you will need to practise in everyday life. You will of course need excellent diction – that is, clarity of speech. Once you've mastered clear speech, the full range of variations in pace of speech is open to you.

Let's take a simple question, 'Are you waiting for someone?', and analyse it for a moment, setting its usage within an imagined context. You're in a bar or a café, seated beside an attractive stranger. You lack confidence in your ability to approach people, but you don't want to appear nervous. First comes the voice. LINT: loudness, inflection, note, and tone. Your voice is going to be quite loud, partly because there's background noise from a jukebox, and partly because you're nervous and lack a degree of control. You've been silently practising this question in your head for the last two minutes. You want to sound relaxed but interested, so your inflection will be a bit varied. You hope that the notes you use will be close to your true root note; you may use higher notes if you're too nervous. You'd like your tone to be fairly relaxed, not too hard. But your body has other ideas: your chest and throat are a bit tight, making it feel as if your voice is centred at the back of your throat, where you can feel a lot of tension.

Now to speech – in this case, pace of speech. Not too fast, not too slow. You want to make a good impression, you want to sound relaxed – 'waitinfosomeone?'

The point I'm re-stating, which applies to all eight characteristics of voice and speech, as well as to all five characteristics of physical behaviour, is that variations occur as a direct result of a person's emotional and psychological state of mind. On a good day, you'll be able to come up with a way of delivering a line which is truthful, interesting and instinctive. On a bad day you'll *sound* truthful, and will be interesting and apparently instinctive. If you're a good actor no-one will ever know the difference.

One more thing to do with pace. In everyday conversation, people vary pace of speech, but they also vary the length of the pauses between the speaking. Someone who is aggressive will typically pause only very briefly in a conversation; indeed they may continually interrupt the other person. A passive or defensive person may pause for some seconds before speaking. It's not difficult to think of psychological reasons why pausing between speech can alter massively from moment to moment; that's real life.

Acting tips

When you, the actor, are presented with a piece of text in which two characters take turns to speak, it can be easy to forget this simple truth about pauses. You learn your lines, you learn your cues, and then you rehearse with the other actor. If you're focused and confident – and if you know your lines and your cues really well – you can 'let go' and discover by instinct how the pauses between the lines should occur. But if anything goes wrong – if either of you has a reason to be tense – then one or both of you will lose the ability to listen and react, which is the essence of good duologue work. What often follows is that the pausing between the lines of text becomes uniform, and thus predictable. I speak, you pretend to listen and react; you speak, I pretend to listen and react. Good actors who get caught in this situation fall back on instinct and make some alteration in the pausing between lines. Lesser actors very quickly become uninteresting.

One way of overcoming this problem is to employ the analogy of a game of tennis. In tennis, each player has the potential to play a shot from the baseline, from the net, or from somewhere in between. A tennis match played entirely 'long distance' – where both players stay back on the baseline, hoping that the other will make a mistake – can be dull indeed to watch. And no tennis match is ever played solely at the net – but when there's a rally at the net it can be really exciting. In a typical match both players alter position frequently and suddenly, hanging back at the baseline one moment, rushing the net at the next. And one of the most exhilarating shots to watch is the long-distance lob, which leaves the opponent stranded or lunging for a return.

For an actor, then, the pacing to avoid is the predictable long-distance 'baseline' delivery which has the same rhythm and length of pause each time. The close-net rally is a brief and frantic exchange of words packed with interruptions. The rest of the scene sees each actor continue to vary pace and pauses according to his own psychological state, which shifts from moment to moment. And the lob? Well, that's the devastating one-liner (statement or question) which leaves the receiver stranded.

Exercises: Solo

The following exercises are quite technical – I'd suggest you use them only to help you to 'get to grips' with pacing and pauses.

1) Below is a section of text from Charles Dickens' *A Christmas Carol*. Read it aloud at a 'normal' pace of speech, using your dictaphone to record your own voice.

   External heat and cold had little influence on Scrooge. No warmth could warm, no wintry weather chill him.

   No wind that blew was bitterer than he, no falling snow was more intent upon its purpose, no pelting rain less open to entreaty.

Foul weather didn't know where to have him.

Nobody ever stopped him in the street to say, with glad-some looks, 'My dear Scrooge, how are you? When will you come to see me?'

No beggars implored him to bestow a trifle, no children asked him what it was o'clock, no man or woman ever once in all his life inquired the way to such and such a place, of Scrooge.

Even the blind men's dogs appeared to know him; and when they saw him coming on, would tug their owners into doorways and up courts; and then would wag their tails as though they said, 'No eye at all is better than an evil eye, dark master!'

Now mark the script in pencil, using the numbers from 1 to 5 to represent pace of speech. If you think a pause is appropriate, write in the letter P (a big P for a longer pause, a small p for a short one). Think of your voice in terms of gears: first gear is very slow, fifth gear is very fast indeed. Make sure that your choice of numbers makes psychological sense from a storyteller's point of view. Record this version on your dictaphone. Play back the two versions for comparison – the one read at your normal pace, and this latest one. Try recording it again, altering the pattern of 'gear changes'.

2) This time use a monologue from a play, which you've divided up into small sections. Go through the speech, marking changes of pace which you feel would occur in response to the character's psychology. Ask yourself questions about the character: is this a difficult thing to say? Does my character mean what they say on this bit, or are they masking something? How do they feel towards the listener? Use a pencil with an eraser – you'll find that your choices change. When you've planned delivery of the speech, record it.

3) This exercise invites you to apply random choices of pace which can sometimes lead to really interesting discoveries. You'll need a die and a pencil, and a second monologue which you've divided into small sections. Toss the die. Working from the start of the speech, note down a number for each small section. Use numbers 1 to 5 as before; if you throw a 6, this is speech so fast that you can barely say the words. Now record the speech, varying pace as planned at random. Listen to the recording: are there moments at which the change of pace is unexpectedly effective?

Exercises: Partnered

1) Repeat exercises 2) and 3) above, but this time use duologues. Again, record your work and play it back. As you listen to it, reflect on any new discoveries regarding use of pace.

2) Exercise using the tennis analogy: a duologue. Select a short duologue from a play which you know well. The scene should be naturalistic in style, and should allow for multiple interpretations. (Harold Pinter's *The Dumb Waiter*, and Beckett's *Waiting for Godot* are good examples.) Discuss an interpretation of the scene which makes psychological sense for each character: you should try to identify what it is that each of your characters wants from the other. (We'll be going into this in detail in the next Section.) Now run the scene, imagining the two characters as 'baseline players', i.e. they each pause before responding to the other. Then reassess the scene so that it can be played 'at the net', i.e. with quick-fire dialogue, your characters often interrupting each other. Now mix it up. Then mix it up again. Discuss how different interpretations affect your feelings towards the other actor's character.

Tool No. 14: Changing Accent

You have an accent – everyone does. No-one is accentless; the most a person can claim is that their accent does not tie them to a specific geographical region, but rather to a social class – for example, the middle-class Standard English accent; or 'hyper English', the traditional accent of the English aristocracy. All other accents link you to a specific geographical region.

Learning a new accent requires a huge amount of time, study and effort. It certainly helps if you're willing to learn the Phonetic Alphabet – that is, the alphabet of sounds which is used in dictionaries to help with pronunciation (see Further Reading). It follows that you need a good 'ear' – an ability to differentiate between sounds. You can still work as an actor if accents are not your strong point – the two Seans, Connery and Bean, seem to have managed pretty well – but if you want to be fully versatile, you do need a good 'ear', and you need to practise using it.

The following is not an attempt to teach you how to do specific accents. Instead, I offer something which I hope is just as useful: a clear insight into how accents vary. Certain patterns recur, and a knowledge of these patterns will take you a long way towards being able to 'crack' most accents.

You'll already be familiar with the simple sounds of verbs – the 'a' in cat, the 'e' in hen, and so on. But you should become familiar also with dipthongs within speech. A dipthong occurs when one verb-sound slides into another, with no consonant in between. Sometimes this switch from one sound to another is very obvious: the word 'boy' is an example of a particularly strong dipthong, which, in standard English, slides from the sound which you get in the middle of the word 'good', to the sound that you get in the middle of the word 'hit'. (Try it.) But if you analyse it carefully, even such a short word as 'go' represents a dipthong, because the pronunciation slides from a sound which is close to the 'u' in the middle of the word 'gun', to a sound which is close to the 'oo' in the middle of the word 'moon' – and this happens almost in an instant. (Try it.) Other dipthongs are found in the centre of the words 'may', and 'hear'. It is these dipthong sounds which often vary the most from accent to accent.

Sometimes a regional accent contains a pronunciation which bears almost no resemblance to the pronunciation of the same sound in standard English. This is when it's especially useful to understand dipthongs. Take, for example, the pronunciation of the word 'now' in a Belfast accent. The dipthong in the middle of this word, as it would be spoken in Standard English, is a sound which slides, approximately, from the sound which you get in the middle of the word 'man', to the sound which you get in the middle of the word 'good'. (Try it.) But when the word 'now' is spoken in a Belfast accent, the dipthong in the middle of the word is totally different. This time, the pronunciation is very close to the dipthong in the word 'boy' (see above). Say out loud the word 'boy', but substitute the letter 'n' for the letter 'b'. That's quite close to how different the pronunciation is.

City accents do tend to have certain general characteristics which differ from those within rural, or country, accents. The clichéd image of the country as a quieter, less feverish environment than the noisy, competitive atmosphere of the city, is pretty well borne out in practice when it comes to accents. City accents such as those from Liverpool, Newcastle, Belfast, and the East End of London tend to have a staccato, broken-up quality. There tends to be quite a lot of use of glottal stops. Pace in city accents is generally very quick. Tone tends to be hard. Diction tends to be poor.

Perhaps the most significant difference between city and rural accents is inflection: if you have a very good 'ear', there's a good chance you'd be able to recognise the major city accents by listening to the inflection pattern alone, without any actual speech. You do, though, have to be careful with inflection. The accents of Birmingham and Liverpool have fairly similar inflection patterns; non-natives often get them mixed up, even though there are significant differences in the way in which specific words are pronounced.

With country accents, pace tends to be slower; tone tends to be softer. The inflection pattern in a country accent tends to have a greater 'musicality': a wider range of notes tends to be used. It's as if the slower pace of a rural lifestyle allows people greater freedom to speak without interruption. City accents, by contrast, seem to hint at the speaker's expectation of being interrupted.

Compare the Belfast Northern Irish accent with a rural Southern Irish accent; the Glasgow Gorbals accent with a Scottish Highland accent. Compare Cockney with Cornish.

Acting tips

If you're keen to learn accents, I'd recommend starting some sort of scrapbook. You could allocate a page to each specific regional accent. For each one you might reflect on the eight key vocal and speech characteristics which vary – LINT PADS. If you can think of any, include the names of famous people, or friends, who are native speakers of each accent. In the Appendix you'll find a sample layout giving the Liverpool accent as an example.

If possible, include recordings of each accent. Some recordings of accents are commercially available, but do be aware that poor or dated versions of accents are worse than useless. The BBC used to produce a good one called 'English, Scottish and Welsh with an Accent': it's a bit dated now, some of the accents have evolved quite a bit since the BBC recording was first made, and you'd struggle to get hold of a copy. There are books dedicated to accents which include CD recordings, but remember that, as a general rule, if all the accents are spoken by the same person then mistakes will inevitably be made. I can recommend two good web links to recordings of native speakers of different accents. In each case you're helpfully given basic information about each speaker. The sites are:

- www.collectbritain.co.uk/collections/dialects This site is part of the service provided by the British Museum in London. Try to seek out speakers who were recorded recently, as many of the ones listed are archive recordings from the last century.
- http://www.ku.edu/%7Eidea/index2.html This one, the International Dialects of English Archive (or IDEA), has been operating since 1997 and is run by the Department of Theatre and Film at the University of Kansas.

acting characters

Exercises: Solo

1) Record your own voice. Just talk about something mundane: what you've done so far today, what you're planning to do later. When you play it back, transcribe a small section of your spoken words onto paper. Leave a gap between lines.

Play that small section back again, and listen carefully to the vocal inflection. Draw a simple pattern above the words you spoke, which shows how the inflection develops and changes during your speech. If you've ever seen this, it should look like a simple version of a transcription of bird-song. Here's a sentence with an example of a basic transcription of an inflection pattern:

I can't see any reason why I should, I really can't.

Repeat the exercise, but record someone else – ideally someone with a different regional accent. Compare the inflection patterns. Certain accents, such as the Birmingham accent, tend to have an inflection pattern which repeats. When you've recorded and transcribed the accent, and 'drawn' a pattern for the vocal inflection, mimic the recorded speaker's accent.

2) Take the simple sentence: 'I can't wait until tomorrow – it's my birthday.' Select two accents, one a city accent and one a country accent. Write the phrase down twice on paper, with a big gap in between. Have a go at each accent. Record your efforts. Repeat the exercise, with another two contrasting accents.

3) Listen to a native speaker using their own accent (e.g. via one of the websites listed on the previous page). Mimic, out loud, what they say, and how they say it; you should be repeating the words only a fraction of a second after the speaker. It takes practice, but it's an excellent way to learn an accent. At first, you can have a transcription of what the person is about to say; with experience, you can just copy them 'live'.

Tool No. 15: Focus on Diction

Diction means clarity of speech. Good diction means speaking clearly while sounding natural. It's an essential skill for an actor: audiences seated in the back row of a big theatre auditorium can only gain a limited amount of information from watching your body; it may be impossible to see the subtleties of your facial expressions. In radio drama there is only your voice. So what you say, and how you say it, is absolutely crucial for good communication.

Contemporary actors working in a climate where the appearance of naturalism is crucial face something of a dilemma. In real life, few people have perfect diction. In real life, regional accents are often hard to fully understand. In real life, psychological stress will often lead to less-than-perfect clarity of speech; and dramas of all sorts tackle stressful moments in the lives of people across the social divide. If you act in a drama, the character you play may well at certain points be under heavy emotional stress. So which is more important – feeling and communicating the emotion using an authentic accent; or speaking the lines clearly?

Of course, it's not a question of either/or. Both are essential. What's required from actors is a skilful blending of two elements: a convincing and appropriate expression of emotion in an authentic-sounding accent, and diction which reaches all of the audience, all of the time. And while you won't need to sound like a graduate of a 1920s elocution class, in a medium such as theatre, where vocal projection is required, you will need to 'add a bit'. So-called 'plosive' sounds in particular (think of explosions), such as p-, d-, k- and g-, need to be 'hit' harder and cleaner than in everyday speech.

These plosives also need to be accurately voiced or unvoiced: d- and t- are identical in terms of how they are produced, yet while d- involves added sound delivered by the vocal cords, t- is made voicelessly. This subtle difference can be especially confusing to an audience if the speaker is using an accent. I've taught speech to acting students from Finland, and the Finnish accent curiously reverses the rules for plosives in Standard English, so that, at its most extreme, the word 'debt' might sound like 'ted'. As with other aspects of voice and speech such as projection, there's a great deal of highly informed and accessible literature available to help actors improve their diction (see Further Reading), so I've elected not to dwell further on it here.

Acting tips

The muscles involved in speech – especially the lips – need to be properly warmed up and actively used, so get into the habit of doing lots of tongue-twisters and pretending to chew very chewy gum. Also, the parts of the body most-used when producing voice (chest, throat, mouth) and associated muscle areas, such as neck and shoulders, need to be kept as relaxed as possible, to avoid 'strangling' the voice with tension, and to facilitate good resonance. The vowel and dipthong sounds in words are the sounds which carry the resonance of the voice. As such they are, in a 'long distance' medium such as theatre, arguably the most important element in transmitting a character's emotional mood; they need to be as unfettered as possible.

In close-up media such as film and television, the viewer expects an intensely realistic style of performance, so any technique you use must be invisible. It's probably best not to think too consciously about diction when acting for camera; my advice here is to focus hard on what your character is fighting for, and just be mindful not to mumble.

Exercises

1) Read aloud a section of text from a story (you could use the excerpt from Dickens' *A Christmas Carol* on pp. 102–3). Imagine you're chewing your words like gum; exaggerate the clarity of your pronunciation by using greater muscularity with your lips, jaw and tongue. Hit the consonants hard but cleanly; work carefully to avoid tightening up your throat. The vowel sounds carry strong resonance and help to express emotion, so keep your voice as free and relaxed as possible.

2) Repeat exercise 1), but this time speak as quickly as you possibly can, and record it. Play it back. How easily can you understand every word? Play it back again, stopping the recording whenever there is a slight lack of clarity. Read other bits of text. Ask someone else to listen to the recordings. Look for a pattern: do you tend to use 'splashy' consonants? Do you tend to 'swallow' certain vowel sounds? Do you use too many glottal stops? When you've seen a pattern, practise altering your diction. Re-record your speech. How clear is it now?

3) Practise daily – and before any performance – these tongue-twisters:

Unique New York, New York unique
A proper cup of coffee in a proper copper coffee pot
Red lorry, yellow lorry
Big black battleships
A proper crop of poppies is a proper poppy crop

and when you become too familiar with them, find and learn new ones.

4) Find and learn a highly emotionally-charged monologue from a play. Spend at least 15 minutes drawing yourself into an appropriate emotional state. Perform the piece, recording it on your dictaphone. Play it back, concentrating just on your diction. Re-record it with improvements.

5) As exercise 4), but this time perform in a large space so that you have to project good diction, while retaining an appropriate emotional state. Leave your dictaphone at a greater distance from you, and play it back to check on diction. Re-record it with improvements.

Tool No. 16: Employing Specials

'Specials' are common idiosyncrasies of speech. Often they're described as speech defects, but they're not really defects – just variations from the standard pronunciation of speech which we call Standard English.

One common Special occurs when speakers substitute the sound 'f' for 'th'; for example, someone will say, 'I fink so'. This particular Special has always been common practice for cockney speakers, but it's now far more widespread, and is particularly common among younger speakers. This might be to do with the spread of the use of cockney, or derivations of the accent: cockney was originally spoken only by people in the East End of London; then it spread wider across that city; and now, characteristics of cockney can be found in regional accents throughout England. The term 'mockney' has been coined to describe people who have adopted a cockney accent, despite being from outside London (the cockney-sounding violinist Nigel Kennedy, for example, comes from the Midlands). Cockney, and mockney, is quite widely spoken by people who have a high profile within youth culture; many presenters, comedians, musicians and models use the accent. This link with youth culture is interesting, because the use of 'f' instead of 'th' is common among young children: by choosing not to adopt what might be considered 'adult' pronunciation of this sound, speakers are, perhaps, rejecting a perceived adult culture in favour of youth culture.

The use of the unvoiced 'f-' instead of the unvoiced 'th-' is echoed in the use of the voiced 'v-' as a replacement for the voiced 'th'. 'Whether', for example, becomes 'wevver'. Note, though, that this altered use is less common at the start of a word; 'this' would not, for example, normally change to 'vis', though it can become 'dis'.

Another Special occurs when people have difficulty pronouncing the strong 'r': the 'r' is pronounced 'w', or on a point somewhere between the two sounds. The word 'worry' becomes 'wowy'. Again, a mild version of this is a common characteristic of a cockney accent; but again, its use has spread to a proportion of speakers of a whole range of regional accents. It's interesting to note that less muscularity is needed for the Specials mentioned so far, compared to the Standard English version.

Another Special is connected to the pronunciation of the 's' sound. Pronunciation hinges on the position of the tongue, especially the tip. The standard pronunciation is achieved by gently placing the tip of the tongue on the lower alveolar ridge (this is the gum area at the front of the mouth, from which the lower front teeth protrude). If you let the tip of the tongue move away from the alveolar ridge, and in particular if you let the tip come fractionally between the teeth, you start to lisp: the 's' sound starts to sound thicker, splashier, and, ultimately, like a 'th' sound.

A further Special occurs when the flow of air is momentarily stopped during speech – the 'glottal stop' which was explored earlier in the book. Once again, cockney is the regional accent in which this Special most frequently occurs; but it's common too in, for example, the Geordie (Newcastle) accent. It's usually a kind of lazy abbreviation: the word 'bottle' loses its central 't' sound and becomes 'bo'l'. Try the phrase 'I've got to get another bottle' – there are at least three glottal stops in that sentence if it's spoken by a Cockney or a Geordie.

If you've realised that your own everyday speech makes use of one or more of these Specials, then, as a transformational character actor, you may have a bit of a problem. In particular if you have a non-standard 's' sound, you may encounter particular difficulty in finding work in recorded media – especially in radio drama and voice-over. Somehow a microphone seems to amplify the 'special' characteristic, and this can be quite jarring on the listener's ear. So do think about getting some one-to-one tuition with a good speech therapist.

An unconscious tendency to use glottal stops in everday speech can be harmful too. Glottal stopping requires the momentary tensing of the throat; breath is trapped, then released. As discussed earlier such tension is not, as a general rule, good for your voice. In theatre you should be aiming for a continuous flow of breath, regulated by your character's thought and feelings. It's easier said than done, but if you can, use glottal stops sparingly on stage.

If you discover that you have further voice or speech training needs, you should ideally enlist the help of a good voice coach.

At the very least you should buy, and use daily, one of the excellent specialist voice and speech books on the market (see Further Reading). The book should break down pronunciation in physical terms, explaining tongue and lip position, for example. Be prepared to start from scratch and work daily on the suggested exercises.

Acting tips

It can make for a really enjoyable challenge to use Specials in your acting. A word or two of warning, though: Specials are, by definition, deviations from 'normal' pronunciation. If you use Specials during speech, you risk harming clear communication. Above all else, your audience needs to know what you're saying.

And don't make things too hard for yourself, either. Using Specials requires hard work in the planning and rehearsal stages, and focus during the performance stage. This takes effort. If you're not careful, your audience will be able to 'see the join' – they'll notice something which is not important. Even worse, it can take so much effort to 'get it right' that the truthfulness and spontaneity of your performance may suffer. Really, *I just fink you've go'o go for it and no' wowy too much ...*

Exercises

1) Start speaking, without any preparation, in your own normal voice. You could just describe what you've done in the last week or so. As you speak, practise spontaneously converting 'th' into 'f' whenever the sound occurs.

2) As exercise 1), this time converting 'r' into 'w'.

3) As above, this time converting your normal 's' sound into a thicker, lisping 's' sound, by minutely protruding your tongue through your teeth. Move the position of your tongue again and discover what other 's' sounds you can create.

4) As above, this time watching out for opportunities to use glottal stops. Speak slowly at first, then repeat words and phrases which seem to lend themselves to the use of glottal stops. To begin with, try out a cockney accent; after that try it with your own, and with other accents.

5) Write a short speech for a character who is to introduce himself on video as part of the process of joining a dating agency. (Perhaps you could have some fun making the person a touch unsuitable as a candidate for finding a partner.) Work through the speech, altering pronunciation in all three of the areas mentioned above.

6) Select a monologue from a 'serious' playscript. Prepare as you did in the last exercise, but this time, be more subtle, and use no more than two Specials. Be careful this time to avoid poking fun at the character. Perform it. Find an unsuspecting audience if you can; find out afterwards if your audience noticed what you were doing, and ask them how it affected their view of your character.

section 6: **inner life**

This final Section is exclusively to do with what goes on inside you – thoughts, emotions, sensations, memories, all linked as they are to the conscious and subconscious mind. We're going to explore how an actor can use his knowledge, skill and imagination to create a sense of inner reality during rehearsal and performance.

Actors 'use' emotion and imagination to varying degrees, depending on their preferred style of acting (e.g. Storyteller or Inhabiter), on the working methods of their director, and on the training they have received. Work on the inner life of a character can be highly rewarding, not least because it's here that truly spontaneous discoveries are most likely to occur.

In this Section we'll be adding the final four new Tools to your repertoire, all of which are forged from the teachings of Stanislavski. Tool Number 17 – The Magic What If? – explores that most basic yet powerful of mental activities, the act of stimulating your imagination. Tool Number 18 – Energising Your Character – examines the benefits of mapping your character's psychological journey through a play, using objectives and barriers. Tool Number 19 – Imagining Sensations – discusses the importance of sensory awareness in performance, and considers how this can best be developed. And Tool Number 20 – Generating Emotion – analyses the importance of stimulating emotion, using psychological spurs such as revisited memories.

Once, when I was rehearsing the role of the seven-year-old twin Eddie for a tour of Willy Russell's *Blood Brothers*, I found inexplicably that I was crying – sobbing, actually. In the scene, Eddie was saying goodbye to his grown-up neighbour, a woman who (unknown to Eddie) also happened to be his natural mother. Something 'clicked' inside me and, in a room full of actors and stage-management crew, I stood sobbing like a baby (or rather, like a seven-year-old child). In subsequent rehearsals this never happened again, but the memory of that emotional outburst always stayed with me, and with the actor playing Mrs Johnstone, so that the scene retained a sense of childish loss as its undercurrent.

Do remember that in the previous Sections we've gone into considerable detail exploring what behavioural signs are out there. These things – and in particular THOSE LINT PADS – give you, the actor, a huge repertoire from which to draw as part of your task of telling stories about the human animal. It's no accident that the 'Inner Life' section comes last; you should now be fully versed in the outer expression of the inner life of a person. Remember, too, that we've already explored the psychological reasons for *why* people's behaviour changes in each of the THOSE LINT PADS areas.

There really is a minefield in this area. Views are polarised, and intensely held. In one corner are those who believe that inner life is the single most important aspect of acting: here you'll be likely to find Lee Strasberg, Michael Chekhov, Konstantin Stanislavski. In support are Method acting 'greats' such as Marlon Brando, Robert De Niro, Daniel Day Lewis, Al Pacino. In the other corner are the advocates of what we might call Representational acting – acting which seems real but does not require constant and intense emotional experience to be effective. Here we might find Laurence Olivier, Michael Caine, Dame Judi Dench – and a younger version of Konstantin Stanislavski. Even Brando, preparing for his Godfather role with cotton wool tucked inside his cheeks, seems to occupy a more central position along with Anthony Hopkins.

So who is right? Neither side? Both sides? It's surely a matter of opinion. But I do believe this: technique and instinct should always be working together. Blending these two things so that you can't see the join, is, for me, the essence of great acting.

So I'm going to focus on offering some ideas for exploring the inner life of a character. As ever, they mostly spring from the mind of Stanislavski. He recognised (and experienced) the need for actors to have a practical process to help them overcome the inherent unreality of acting: the requirement to act 'on cue' between, say, 7.30pm and 10pm; the demand to do so nightly, for perhaps as long as a year, using the same words every time; and the unremitting falseness of a situation whereby you stand on a stage trying to ignore both your audience, and the assistant stage manager perched in the wings.

You'll notice, by the way, a slight change in format in this final Section. The 'Acting tips' have been incorporated into the main text, simply because we're now looking specifically at the skill of acting (so you could say that everything you're about to read represents acting tips). Also, each sub-section now includes exercises and activities within the text, rather than at the end. This means that as a reader you can exercise your imagination 'as you go', which better suits the spirit of this Section. After all, as you sit, seemingly innocently reading this Section, how many of the people nearby know what you're really up to?

Tool No. 17: The Magic What If?

The final key to keeping your acting as truthful as possible is, of course, active use of your imagination. Interestingly, active imagining is used a lot these days by those other performers who work under heavy psychological and physical pressure – sportsmen and women. Sprinters and tennis players use it (though they call it visualisation) – visualising, as they do, that moment when they reach the tape in first place, or when they deliver a match-winning first-serve ace. And it works (usually).

Actors imagine too, of course; it's at the very heart of what they do. To be a good actor, you need to be open and responsive to your imagination. Stanislavski's most simple concept is also, I think, his most effective – the so-called 'Magic If'. What if – ? This simple phrase is a wonderfully direct challenge to that part of you which enjoyed playing games of imagination as a child. In *An Actor Prepares*, Stanislavski sets up a hugely powerful 'what if' which has the threat of a deranged would-be killer outside the room. Wherever you are as you read this, imagine that now: you (not a character, but the real you) are at risk of attack from a person nearby who has the means to kill you. What do you feel?

Rather cleverly, that no longer becomes the key question. What's more important is, what should you do? How do you ensure your survival? What about loved ones nearby, what can you do to protect them? What if the would-be killer hasn't seen you, and if you keep still they may just go away? Use your imagination now to focus hard on that. As you do so, your mind will be whirring with thoughts and feelings, but your body will be pretty well still. You will be experiencing inner life.

Of course, you don't have to be still to experience inner life; indeed, Section Three of this book explored in some detail how even minor tensions and movements give out clues. You should have learned, through that earlier Section on 'The Body', what are the external signs of a person's thoughts and feelings. What we're considering now, is how an imagined stimulus (an image or a memory, for example) can spur you on to physical action. We're going 'inside the character' to discover how things you imagine, while in character, do actually prompt a spontaneous physical expression.

Back to the deranged would-be killer for a moment. You're keeping as still as possible in the hope that he won't see you and will go away. You just want him to go away. What are you feeling? Who cares, frankly. You just want him to go away. But he's still there, edging around, peering in your direction. You hear a shout, or a bang. Has he seen you? If he has, what now? You need an escape route. How well do you know this place? How far is it to safety and help? Would it be safer to sit it out and try to reason with him? How are you feeling? (Not great, actually, you think to yourself, but can we discuss that later?)

Life isn't always that dramatic, of course, but we all face similar challenges when we find ourselves on a crash-course towards some-one we really want to avoid. And while they're not threatening to kill you, they might inadvertently bore you to death. Look again at the questions in the paragraph above – they still apply. If you're in company now as you're reading this, select someone nearby as a person you desperately want to avoid (you'll need to create a reason which relates to your social relationship with them). Keeping your physical movement as minimal as possible, concen-trate hard on what action you will take if they approach you.

Something which Stanislavski bravely asserted, and which I've hinted at in the scenarios described above, is that feelings – emotions – are not things that you should plan in advance. Being able to act intense emotions 'on cue' is sometimes seen as the mark of a great actor, but in truth, while such acting can at best be very moving, at worst it can be an unwelcome party trick which detracts from the story.

Still, it can be very tempting to map out a character's progress through a play by trying to pin down his changing emotions. You think to yourself, 'he's angry at this point', or 'he was amused before but now he's getting upset'. Resist. If you build a perform-ance from predetermined emotions, your acting will become generalised, predictable, and unresponsive to the other actors. And you set yourself up to fail ('damn, I didn't cry on that bit AGAIN!'). Look at Hamlet. In his story he spends much of his time failing to act; he keeps discovering or inventing reasons why he should hold back. It's tempting to label him as 'depressed', 'bitter', 'suicidal' even. But play him that way and after two hours your audience will be egging him on to do it! Better instead to acknowledge Shakespeare's talent for creating believ-able and sophisticated characters, who act in response to their changing circumstances – and to work out what Hamlet is thinking. After all, who told the grieving Hamlet that his uncle murdered his father? A ghost, that's who. I don't know about you, but I'd need a bit more to go on before killing my uncle – especially if he's making an effort to be nice to me. I'd need to do some soul-searching, and some digging.

If active imagining is so important for actors, how, then, can you develop your imagination? Simple: through practice. Play 'what if – ?' games as you go about your daily business, and especially when you're bored (when your mind is looking for a stimulus). Where should you start? Wherever you like. You could, though, do a lot worse than revisiting some of the exercises in earlier Sections of this book, and adding a powerful 'what if – ?' to the scenario.

Example: Natasha from *Three Sisters*

Read and rehearse this longer scene below from Act Three. For the scene to work fully for both actors and audience, there should initially be a strong sense of imminent threat (from fire which has been sweeping through the town). The stress of this situation doubtless contributes to Natasha losing her temper so violently later in the scene. As actors rehearsing the scene, you should start by asking yourself, 'What if, while we are running the scene, there is a genuine threat of fire outside the building?' Try alternatives. Have you ever been in a place where there was a threat of natural disaster, or terrorism? If so, try to recall the detail of that experience, what you wanted, what you actually did. Add it to the mix as you imagine the fire. If not – well, it is a *magic* if. Be as focused as possible – and imagine it.

[NATASHA comes in.]

NATASHA

They're talking about setting up a committee to help the victims of the fire. What do you think? It's a splendid idea. Of course we should help the poor, it's the duty of the rich. Bobik and little Sophie are sleeping, fast asleep as if nothing was wrong. There's so many people around, the house is full of them, everywhere you go. There's a 'flu epidemic in the town now. I'm frightened the children may catch it.

OLGA *[Not listening]*

We can't see the fire in this room, it's quiet here.

NATASHA

Yes ... I suppose I look a mess. *[Before the mirror]* They say I'm putting on weight. It's not true! Absolutely not. Masha's asleep; the poor thing's worn out ... *[Coldly, to ANFISA]* Don't you dare be seated in my presence! Get up! Out! *[Exit ANFISA; a pause]* I don't understand what makes you keep that old woman on!

OLGA *[Confused]*

Sorry, I don't understand ...

NATASHA

She's no use here. She's a peasant, she ought to live in the country ... Spoiling her, I call it! I need order in the house! We can't have any malingerers here. *[Strokes Olga's cheek]* You're tired, poor thing! Our headmistress is tired! When my little Sophie grows up and goes to school I shall be afraid of you.

OLGA

I shan't be headmistress.

NATASHA

They're appointing you, Olga. It's settled.

OLGA

I'll refuse the post. I can't ... I'm not strong enough ... *[Drinks a glass of water]* You were so rude to Nanny just now ... I'm sorry. I can't bear it ... I feel faint ...

NATASHA *[Agitated]*

I'm sorry, Olga, forgive me ... I didn't mean to upset you.

[MASHA gets up, collects a pillow and exits angrily.]

OLGA

You have to understand, dear ... perhaps we've been brought up rather oddly, but I can't bear that. Such behaviour gets me down. I get ill ... I feel drained.

NATASHA

I'm sorry, forgive me ... *[Embraces her.]*

OLGA

The least bit of rudeness, the slightest of harsh words, upsets me.

NATASHA

I do speak out of turn, it's true, but you must agree, dear, that she could just as easily live in the country.

OLGA

She's been with us for thirty years.

NATASHA

But she can't work any more. Either I don't understand you, or you don't want to understand me. She's no longer fit for work, she just sleeps or sits about.

OLGA

Then let her sit!

NATASHA *[Surprised]*

What do you mean? She's a servant. *[Tearfully]* I don't understand you, Olga. I've got a nanny, a wet-nurse, we've a cook, a housemaid ... what do we want that old woman for as well? What use is she?

[Distant fire-alarm is heard]

OLGA

I've aged ten years to-night.

NATASHA

We must come to some arrangement, Olga. Your place is the school, mine – the home. You devote yourself to teaching, I look after the household. And if I say something about servants, then I know what I am talking about; I do know what I am talking about ... And by to-morrow there'll be no more of that old thief, that old hag ... *[Stamping]* that old witch! And don't you dare annoy me! Don't you dare! *[Calming herself]* Really, Olga, if you don't move downstairs, we'll be quarrelling endlessly. This is terrible.

[Enter KULIGIN, MASHA's husband]

KULIGIN

Where's Masha? It's time we went home. The fire seems to be dying down. *[Stretches himself]* Only one district has burnt down, but there was such a wind that it looked like the whole town was going to go up. *[Sits]* I'm worn out. Dear Olga ... I often think that if it hadn't been for Masha, I would have married you. You're so nice ... I'm absolutely worn out. *[Listens.]*

OLGA

What is it?

KULIGIN

The doctor – he's been drinking hard; he's completely drunk. Perhaps he's done it on purpose! *[Gets up]* He's coming ... Do you hear him? *[Laughs]* What a man ... really ... I'll hide. *[Goes to the cupboard and stands in the corner]* What a rogue.

OLGA

He hasn't touched a drop in two years, and now he suddenly goes and gets drunk ...

[Retires with NATASHA to the far end of the room.]

Tool No. 18: Energising Your Character
Units and objectives

At any given moment in a well-written play, then, a character is up to something: it's what characters do to keep busy, to fill out their lives. (People, of course, are just the same.) In a play, it's what keeps the story moving forwards.

The way in which a character's circumstances change, and how your character responds to the changes, energises your character within the story of the play. If you can imagine yourself into the world, and the story, of your character – and if you can do so at each point in the play, so that at each point you know what your character is up to – then you can create a useable map for your character's journey. Stanislavski's solution – another brilliantly simple device – was to divide up the play into small sections, or units, in which an actor's character is fighting for something specific. This 'want', he called an Objective.

To map out the units in a play, go back first to your Character Profile Sheet and identify (or remind yourself) what is your character's **Lifetime Objective**. Look again too at their **Favourite Fantasy**. Lodge these two elements in your mind as you move to the next stage; pretty well everything you come up with should be somehow connected with your character's desire for those two lifetime goals.

Next, go through your script from the start of the play, marking your script in pencil each time there is significant change in circumstances. Often this means that a character in the story enters or leaves; but it can also mean that one character has started to push for something new within the scene. Every time something significant changes, there's an effect on the characters in the scene: if someone enters, you have to make an instant assessment of how to react to their presence – do you need to ask them something, do you want them to go away, or what? If someone leaves, you can perhaps relax and re-think your plans, or you can talk about them. Each action has a reaction. The same is true for the more subtle changes: if your character was trying to make another character laugh, and they do laugh, you've got what you wanted; so look for the next thing you want. If your character fails to make the other character laugh, what do you do instead? It may be that your character tries a different tack to make them laugh, in which case you're still in the same unit; or they may give up and fight for something new, which means that your next unit has begun.

Once you've identified the units, number them from Unit 1 upwards. (I tend to identify an average of two or three per page, but they can vary from a tiny unit which takes place before anyone speaks, to perhaps two pages of intensive dialogue.) After that, the process is essentially quite simple, and is certainly instinctive: you view each unit from each character's perspective; then you get inside your own character's heart and head to find out what they are up to. When you've found each discrete 'want' – your character's objective in each unit – lodge it firmly in your own heart and mind, remembering it always with the phrase 'I want ...'. A word of advice – don't be vague. Make each objective specific, and playable. 'I want you to like me' is vague, and hard to play. 'I want to make you smile' is specific, and suggests actions you might take to achieve it. Another word of advice – be instinctive when deciding when a unit changes. This is not a science. If you think you may have changed unit numbers too soon – well, that's why you're using a pencil. And anyway Unit 15 could easily vanish or be split into Units 15a and 15b at a later point. If you're not sure if there's a change in unit, let the unit continue.

Do this with a small section of a play, and you have a short series of specific objectives to fight for, a focus for your energies onstage. Do this with the full script, and you will have sketched out a simple psychological map to follow throughout the whole journey of the play.

How do you go about achieving your objectives? I feel that's for you to explore in the rehearsal room. You could identify different methods for attempting an objective. If your aim is, 'I want to make you smile', how do you fight to achieve it? You could grin. You could pull a silly face. You could flatter warmly. Such alternative 'actions' can be plotted too if that's your preference; my feeling is that if you plan in this much detail you can start to deny yourself the space to be spontaneous. Your map can become too detailed.

Barriers

Of course it's all very well wanting something, but what if you don't get it? Life, someone said, is what happens to us when we're looking the other way. So it is too with characters. If things get in the way, then that in itself can be fascinating. Look again at that bit three paragraphs above. The objective was 'I want to make you smile'. Even more interesting might be 'I want to kiss you': assuming that (for now at least) you have to settle for less, that struggle in itself – the sense that things are getting in the way – can give your acting real focus.

The things that are getting in the way are quite simply barriers. Barriers can be real, physical barriers: Juliet longs for Romeo ('Come, Romeo!'), but as far as she can tell he's simply not there, so the barrier is the distance between them. Then there are psychological barriers (just ask Hamlet, whose only source as to who killed his father is, as I said earlier, a ghost).

It's important not to gloss over this 'barriers' aspect of a character's inner life. I'm all for actors imagining things beyond the lines and the stage directions; anything which helps the actor believe in his character's given circumstances can surely only be positive. Just thinking it, though, doesn't mean that the audience sees it too. But when you translate what you're thinking and feeling into an active 'want' – when you make an active effort to achieve an objective – then that battle for something you want is something the audience can observe, and can try to understand. The process of 'playing' a character's active objective represents the crucial link between what you're thinking and feeling, and what your audience can witness. And the barriers raise the stakes. When audiences see people struggling to achieve something, it pulls harder on their sense of empathy. By making imaginative use of objectives and barriers, you're acting with focus and truthfulness, you're actively telling the story of the play, and you're doing so while staying fully 'in character'.

Let's imagine for a moment that you're not reading a book, but are listening to me giving a lecture. We're in a classroom which contains me, you, and a dozen or so other acting students. You decide the time, place, and who the people are in the group.

The subject of the lecture is 'objectives and barriers'. I've spoken the words above out loud, the ones which begin after the headline, 'Energising your character'. You're keen to learn (or refresh); I'm keen to share the knowledge. Let's place a few more details in to spice things up.

I'm here as a guest lecturer, and this is the first time we've been in class together, so although I've taken a register I don't really know your names. You learned a bit about 'objectives' from a favourite teacher a year ago, but didn't fully grasp it. There was a party last night and some of the other actors in the room are trying to hide the after-effects; three who were at the party are absent. You can vaguely hear singing in a neighbouring room, a recent song from the charts.

Let's think through the possible consequences of these new given circumstances.

I want to teach, and you want to learn. But three of your fellow actors didn't even turn in today. I know this, because I've marked them absent on my workshop register. So no matter how keen I am to teach them, their absence is a solid physical barrier to achieving this. I can leave notes for them, they could even watch a video of the lecture, but I've no guarantee that notes will be read or video watched, so as far as those three are concerned, I've failed in my goal.

Another student actor is suffering a physical barrier, because English is his second language and he's having trouble understanding my accent and my fast pace of speech (I'm a bit nervous). The actor could ask me to slow down, but he's embarrassed at his own sense of inadequacy so he keeps quiet; his embarrassment is a psychological barrier which prevents him from learning. Anyway, he was at the lecture given by your favourite teacher a year ago and he felt he'd grasped the concepts well. That teacher had referred to 'obstacles' rather than barriers, which now seems confusing, so this student with limited English has decided to stick with his prior knowledge and switch off in class, while politely pretending to listen. I, meanwhile, as an experienced teacher, have noticed that this student is showing signs of what I'm labelling NDS – nodding dog syndrome. Whatever I say, as soon as our eyes meet he nods reassuringly. I know there's a possible problem but without knowing the group better I don't know what the problem is; I'm guessing he was at a party last night (he wasn't).

I decide to go over the main points of the lecture again in brief so that everyone can take something away from the class. As soon as I do so I sense that a couple of the more engaged listeners have 'dropped out', and I may struggle to get them back. Meanwhile the singer in the next room continues to sing the recent chart song loud enough for us all to hear. To me, the singing is an annoying physical barrier – I have to raise my voice to compete. To you, it's a psychological barrier – the song reminds you of something special which happened during your last holiday.

Examples of both physical and psychological barriers can be found pretty well at any point in any play. I'd suggest, though, that you don't write them into your script – yet. Barriers can often be things which only reveal themselves when you're actually on your feet running the scene. Let's say you've mapped out the units, and come up with an Objective – a 'want' – at the start of each unit. Next, get up on your feet, script in hand. Have a go at 'walking' a few units; fight for each objective as it changes. Where are the problems? New ones may present themselves. 'I can't say this to my friend because that person by the door can hear too.'

'I want him to go but he's already taking his coat off.' 'I want him to smile but he's not even looking at me.'

Units, objectives and barriers – an exercise

Here's a bit of dialogue. You've seen it already earlier in the book. Re-read it now, and see if you can identify any changes in unit; any objectives; any physical barriers; any psychological barriers. I've written this to be intentionally vague, so that you can apply more than one interpretation to it:

A: Hello.

B: Hello.

A: Cold isn't it?

B: It is.

A: Have we met before?

B: Have we? I don't know.

A: I think we have.

B: When?

A: I don't know.

B: No.

Here's one possible deconstruction of the interaction. Read it through once, then try 'playing' each character:

A park bench. B, who is attractive and has a foreign appearance, is seated at one end. B is listening to music via tiny headphones.

Unit 1:

A approaches B and sits.

A first wants to know if B speaks English. Physical barrier = B is listening to music and can't hear. Psychological barrier = B is also showing subtle non-verbal communication which indicates a desire for privacy.

B wants to be left alone to think. Physical barrier = A has just sat on end of bench. Psychological barrier = B has been brought up to be polite to strangers.

A: *(leaning into view, loudly)* Hello.

B: *(removing headphones while turning very slightly away from A)* Hello.

Unit 2:

A wants eye contact with B. Physical barrier = B is now turned slightly further away. Psychological barrier = B's slight turn has dented A's confidence.

B still wants to be left alone. Physical barrier = A is still there. Psychological barrier = A's voice sounds friendly.

A: Cold isn't it?

B: It is.

A: Have we met before?

B: Have we? *(turns to look at A)* I don't know.

Unit 3:

> A wants to make B smile. No physical barrier. Psychological barrier = B seems shy of full eye contact.
>
> B still wants to be left alone. Physical barrier = A is still there. Psychological barrier = A looks attractive.
>
> **A:** I think we have.
>
> **B:** When?
>
> **A:** *(pulling a face which says, 'My memory is hopeless!')* I don't know.
>
> **B:** *(smiling)* No.

What I've added into the scene, then, are simply the thoughts and desires that drive each of the two characters in the small section shown. It might look a bit daunting – I've added quite a lot of background. But it doesn't have to be as detailed as that. Here's an abbreviated version, which just the actor playing A might use:

> A park bench.

Unit 1:

> *(Sit on end)*
>
> (Obj = 'B – speak!'. Phys B = walkman. Psych B = 'Garbo' body lang.)
>
> **A:** Hello.
>
> **B:** Hello.

Unit 2:

(Obj = 'look at me!' Phys B = B turned away. Psych B = I'm losing confidence.)

A: Cold isn't it?

B: It is.

A: Have we met before?

B: Have we? I don't know.

Unit 3:

(Obj = 'smile!' Psych B = A is shy with eye contact.)

A: I think we have.

B: When?

A: I don't know. *(show jokey 'My memory is hopeless!')*

B: No.

So you can still plan your map of Units/Objectives/Barriers without drowning in words. You simply work out each of your character's specific objectives, physical barriers, and psychological barriers at each point in the play, and you'll be well on your way to a focused performance. Apply that knowledge bravely but sensitively in rehearsal, and be open to changes (keep using a pencil), and you'll writing yourself a map for a secure first night.

Incidentally, if you're thinking that three units in the space of ten lines is quite a lot of units, it's worth noting that the circumstances in a scene do basically dictate the number of units. One last look at the lines. This time, the scenario is that

B is happily reading, while A approaches, simply thinking that he recognises B:

Unit 1:

> A wants to know if B is an acquaintance from some years ago. Physical barrier = B's face is hard to see as B is reading. Psychological barrier = A thinks he may have made a mistake.
>
> B wants to carry on reading. No physical barrier; psychological barrier is that A seems to want to talk.
>
> **A:** Hello.
>
> **B:** Hello.
>
> **A:** Cold isn't it?
>
> **B:** It is.
>
> **A:** Have we met before?
>
> **B:** Have we? I don't know.
>
> **A:** I think we have.
>
> **B:** When?
>
> **A:** I don't know.
>
> **B:** No.

In this case the 'wants' stay the same for both characters, so there's no change in unit. Don't take my word for it – have a go.

Tool No. 19: Imagining Sensations

The five senses – sight, hearing, touch, taste and smell – are, of course, not the same as the emotions. They are linked, in that an intense sensory experience may well stimulate a strong emotional response; for example, sudden pain can cause fear or anger. But mild 'background' sensory stimulation is around us all the time, and much of it remains just that – background. As I write this, if I listen, I can hear a cartoon showing on the television in another room, I can hear a song playing on the radio in the kitchen, a jet plane is flying overhead, and my neighbour is mowing her lawn. I'm looking at my computer screen and keyboard in turn, but my peripheral vision tells me that my dog is lying in the hallway, sleeping soundly. I've just enjoyed a shortbread biscuit, and I'm about to take a sip of tea. The keyboard sits on a cold metal pull-out drawer on which I rest my hands between typing; when I'm thinking I stroke my chin, which is unshaven. The dog has just rolled onto his back into a funny position which makes him look like he's just fallen off the ceiling. My senses are being bombarded with 'background' stimulation, but none of it is enough to make me break off writing. (Tell a lie – I've just had a sip of tea ... delicious.)

I've just saved progress on my computer and the programme I'm using has answered my command to 'Save' with a chirpy note – 'bling!' – which sounds like some sort of flourish. Now I think about it, that 'bling!' is an important part of the writing process; it tells me I'm making progress and so encourages me to write a bit more. Put simply, the effect is as follows:

Sensory stimulus *(causes an)* emotional reaction *(which encourages)* action

'Bling!'   I'm pleased with progress   write a bit more

The point, though, is this. While an actor's awareness of his five senses is important, you mustn't let your sensory awareness dominate when it's not of real significance to the story you're helping to tell. Look again at the (real) scene I've just described as I sat typing a few minutes ago. If this was a scene in a film, what aspects of the scene would be most important for the audience? Of course, it depends on the story and the character. If the character is a writer who cannot tear himself away from his writing, then the presence of an ignored dog who is getting restless tells you something about the writer's state of mind. If the character is a spy who is accessing someone else's computer, then the chin-stroking might be helpful in revealing the pressure on him. Some of the other sensory details – the biscuit, the lawnmower, the cold metal, even (in this case) the dog – are probably irrelevant distractions to both actor and audience. Of course, on a film set the actor is already coping with a range of pressures – not the least of which is the presence of a great gang of crew members, watching only to see that their 'bit' of the process is working well. You're worrying about continuity, trying to remember lines, limiting your movement so that you don't cast a shadow on your fellow actor, trying to fight for your 'want' despite the (in-character) barriers which block your way. If you don't notice the lawnmower (which isn't really) buzzing away in the background, whisper it, but no-one will notice or even care.

You're an actor, not a member of the X-Men. Your most impressive powers are that you imagine things in a way that other people find accessible. I like that mnemonic KISS – keep it simple, stupid. Don't let yourself (or other people) clog up your creative faculty – your ability to transmit what you imagine. You can't, for example, play two objectives – two 'wants' – simultaneously. (If you're stuck choosing between two, chances are that one of them is actually a barrier.) You can't transmit everything that is happening to your senses when 'in character'; or, rather, it doesn't help if you try too hard to do so. Prioritise. If the sensory stimulus is essentially 'background', leave it there. If it's very much relevant to the story – and especially, if the sensory stimulus prompts an emotion which prompts a desire for action ('bling!') – then imagine it, and imagine it hard.

How hard do you have to work to imagine such sensory stimuli? To some extent, actors in the 21st century are spoiled compared to those of a hundred or more years ago. In the late 19th century the playwright August Strindberg wrote how he longed for a theatre in which the set for a kitchen might consist of more than just 'painted pots and pans', lit by distorting footlights. The quick march towards the realism which Strindberg sought has now left us with a theatre, and of course a world of film and television, in which actors are surrounded by sets, costumes, hairstyles and so on of the most acute realism. To a high degree you can just open up your senses to the sights and sounds which the designers and crew have created for you.

When is this not the case? Interestingly, those worlds in which transformational character acting is still valued, also tend to be the areas in which the actor has to make the effort to imagine the things which stimulate his senses. The small-cast plays of Steven Berkoff and John Godber often require the actors to evoke a world full of sights, sounds, textures, tastes and smells. Radio plays rely heavily on the actors allowing their voices to be infused with imagined images, tastes, smells. And the language of William Shakespeare is painstakingly designed to fill the heads of audiences with sensory stimuli, whether it be Caliban's 'thousand twangling instruments' which hum about his ears, or any one of the myriad images which flash shape, colour and emotion into the listener's mind.

So how can you develop your ability to imagine sensory stimuli? As part of the process of training to be an actor, quite a lot of time should be spent on improvisations which stimulate your five senses. When I was at drama school in England we did a lot of this. We'd be survivors of a plane crash in the desert, suffering pain from our injuries, intense heat from the wind and sun, thirst from lack of water. Or we'd be homeless people settling down to sleep in a city square, suffering hunger from lack of food, cold from the snow and wind; we'd huddle together for warmth. Or we'd be aliens dropped in from another galaxy, and we'd have perhaps no sight but a really good sense of hearing, and we'd have a unique way of moving. Or we'd be animals caged in a zoo, left for the night to hear and smell the threats and temptations which came on the air to our ears and our noses.

Such improvisations are invaluable in keeping your imagination well-exercised. They should take place behind closed doors, with no formal audience. They should be open-ended, so that no story, no 'result' is demanded of you. The purpose is simply to practise imagining things which stimulate your senses. They're great fun – serious and valuable, but also fun and childlike.

Just as important are solo exercises, ideally watched by your fellow acting students. You might imagine being alone in your home – getting dressed, shaving, dancing to music, eating, just doing everyday things. The aim is to achieve Stanislavski's state of 'solitude in public', by being as focused as possible on the things within the imagined world, unaware of the observers.

But of course to get fit you don't have to just exercise in the gym. So stretch your imagination 'muscles' all the time with spontaneous 'what if?' games. What if you suddenly smell a terrible odour? What if someone really, really attractive smiles at you? What if you unexpectedly 'hear' a song on the 'radio' which reminds you of a special memory? What if, when you're feeling low, a friend arrives and wraps their arms around you?

Example: Natasha from *Three Sisters*

Read and rehearse this short scene below from Act Four. There's an undercurrent of loss as they distantly hear soldiers – for so long the lifeblood of the place – leaving the town. Also, some distance away, an unseen duel is scheduled between the Baron TUZENBACH and SOLENI, which could prove fatal (you don't yet know that it will). There's a spectrum of sensory stimuli to be imagined and explored: 'live' sights (e.g. Natasha appearing at a window above, the children, the newspaper) and sounds (e.g. distant marching, birds, crying, music playing), plus remembered sensations, such as tastes and smells and extreme cold. Take the trouble to revisit your own memories of the same, or of similar, experiences and sensations. Take your time. When you've arrived at a focused state of mind – one in which these experiences and sensory stimuli are available to your imagination – you're ready to begin the scene.

ANDREI

I hate the life I have now, but when I think of the future, how good it looks! I feel so light, so free; there's a glimmer in the distance, I can see freedom. I see myself and my children freeing ourselves from idleness, from stale beer, from goose and cabbage, from after-dinner naps ...

FERAPONT

They say two thousand people froze to death. People were scared stiff. In Petersburg or Moscow, I don't remember which.

ANDREI *[Overcome by a tender emotion]*

My dear sisters, my beautiful sisters! *[Crying]* Masha, my dear ...

NATASHA *[At the window]*

Who's making all the noise out here? Is that you, Andrei? You'll wake little Sophie. – Il ne faut pas faire du bruit, la Sophie est dormée deja. Vous êtes un ours. – *[Angrily]* If you want to talk, then give the pram to somebody else. Ferapont, take the pram!

FERAPONT

Yes ma'am. *[Takes the pram]*

ANDREI *[Confused]*

I was talking quietly.

NATASHA *[At the window, nursing her boy]*

Bobik! Naughty Bobik! Bad little Bobik!

ANDREI *[Looking through the papers]*

All right, I'll look them over and sign where necessary, and you can take them back to the council offices ...

[*Goes into house reading papers; FERAPONT takes the pram upstage to the back of the garden.*]

NATASHA [*At the window*]

Bobik, what's your mummy's name? Clever boy! And who's this? That's Aunt Olga. Say to your aunt, 'Hello, Olga!'

[*Two wandering musicians, a man and a girl, are playing on a violin and a harp. VERSHININ, OLGA, and ANFISA come out of the house and listen for a minute in silence; IRINA goes up to them.*]

Tool No. 20: Generating Emotion

I know. Emotion is not necessarily something you can just generate, like electricity. And frankly actors are set up to fail in this area, so long as directors, or acting teachers, or audience members demand that an actor should burst into tears on cue like some performing sideshow attraction. (An actor in a recent hit TV series described this as being a regular part of her previous role in a daytime 'soap' in the USA. She 'dreaded' the scenes that called for it. You might know the very witty song in the musical *A Chorus Line*, in which Diana Morales, a beleaguered student actor, lists the wild imaginary journeys her acting teacher forces her class to take. She confesses darkly that at every turn 'I felt nothing!'.)

It's best not to strain and stretch to 'feel' emotion. Instead, try sticking with the 'units' method explored earlier in this Section. Work out a route through the story by identifying what it is, at each point, that your character is fighting for (your objective), and what gets in the way (the barriers). Then plough your energies into imagining these things, and strive for real moment-by-moment interaction with your fellow actor(s). You should become affectively drawn into that moment of the story – with real emotion being the result. That's what happened to me when I burst into tears while rehearsing *Blood Brothers*.

What if you don't feel the emotion? Well, if you've read this book from the start, and performed the exercises, you will now also be armed with a sophisticated practical knowledge of human non-verbal and verbal communication, much of which results from experiencing (or trying to hide) emotion. This stuff is invaluable in rehearsal, when you're exploring relationships and developing your character. But it can also rescue you in performance. Your knowledge is an aspect of your 'technique' – something to fall back on. And the chances are that if you find yourself onstage without any true sense of emotion ('up against the wall Smith! You are charged with being onstage with no emotions whatsoever!') then you can use your knowledge to help you. Just consciously take on the appropriate tension, eye contact, pace of speech, and your mind will 'feel' something going on and reconnect you to a spontaneous emotional state. And if it doesn't – it's unlikely anyone will notice, because the behavioural side of your performance, meaning that which the audience can observe, looks right. Think of your knowledge as your emergency jump-leads; carry a set with you at all times.

Stanislavski recognised that emotions are difficult to lasso and to harness, especially when a role has been performed repeatedly for some months. As an actor he had a bit of a crisis of confidence at one point and decided that the goal, the way forwards, was to feel real emotion at all times. Psychiatry and Psychoanalysis were growing fast at this point; the concept of the 'subconscious' was becoming an accepted scientific truism. Stanislavski pondered how the emotions seem somehow to be anchored in our subconscious selves. His ever-evolving System started to focus more and more on using 'conscious means [to] reach the subconscious'. He started experimenting with 'emotion memory'.

Essentially, emotion-memory exercises require the actor to be encouraged to remember emotional experiences, so that the remembered emotion resurfaces. Of course, this is something which patients do when undergoing therapy with a psychiatrist or a psychoanalyst. You've probably spotted a danger here: these latter two professions require (mostly) that a patient's psychological state is paramount, and that all work takes place in a safe and confidential environment.

Actors, as we know, are all mad. Yet despite this, those untrained in how to work with traumatised people are allowed to tear the actors' innermost traumas from their scarred subconsciousness – and they do so in public. And more often than not, the actors thank them for it. (Absolute proof of madness, you might say.)

There's no doubt that emotion-memory exercises are valuable, in that they 'stretch' an actor. It's usually a pleasant shock for an actor to experience, in a workshop situation, the spontaneous arrival of an intense emotion, especially if the emotion is one which they secretly struggle to generate.

But as an acting teacher I can be a bit uncomfortable with my position as midwife to the revisiting of intense emotional memories. I don't want to leave anyone feeling depressed and saddened as they sit in their bedroom later that night, their long-buried traumas swirling around them. So I always set a couple of ground rules which help to keep our status as equal as possible.

Firstly, you, the student, get to choose the memory. Secondly, you decide whether real names are used. Thirdly, either of us can end the activity as and when we think it necessary. Fourthly, the other student actors get to watch (acting is a public activity). And fifthly, everyone has to agree that what is revealed during the workshop remains strictly confidential. I find that if such a workshop is explained, carefully managed, allowed its own pace, and with the five rules strictly adhered to, then the outcome is successful for all. Acting students become more able to emote spontaneously, and to do so in front of others; and there's a greater sense of trust between us all.

As ever, though, there are doubts as to the value and necessity of emotion-memory exercises. Stanislavski was caught out when one of his own actors became highly emotional when recalling the funeral of his recently deceased father. Deeply moved, Stanislavski comforted the performer – only to learn that the actor's father was still very much alive. (The actor had used his imagination.) Interestingly, that actor, Michael Chekhov, later became something of an acting guru in the United States; he's probably best-known for the technique of the 'psychological gesture', whereby a person's psychological state is given expression through a seemingly unconscious physical gesture.

Example: Natasha from *Three Sisters*

Read and rehearse the short section of the scene below from Act Four. In this final sequence at the end of the play there's a sense that Natasha is now in full control, confidently appointing her lover Protopopov, as well as her husband Andrei, to babysitting duty, planning bold changes to the garden, and, in a neat reversal, even daring to criticise Irina's dress sense. It's been a long journey for Natasha, and we hear her in full 'stream of consciousness' mode as she speaks aloud her plans. What, though, are the other characters thinking but not saying?

As you plan for rehearsal, use the full range of techniques described above – identifying units, clarifying objectives, establishing physical and psychological barriers – and also hunting for moments from your own experience which 'chime' emotionally. Be imaginative in looking for experiences from your own life, which you could draw on. Have you, for instance, ever 'got your own back' on a bully? How did you feel about it afterwards? A word or two of warning. You'll need to match Chekhov's understanding of the mind to work out what's really going on in this tiny sequence; Chekhov is after all the master of subtext, in that his characters often seem to be saying one thing, while thinking something related, but different. Remember too that in real life people don't plan monologues; they become monologues because other people decide not to speak. Make sure you link your ideas back to Natasha's prior experiences: refer for one last time to her Character Profile Sheet in the Appendix.

When you think you're ready, set to work, using all the force of your imagination.

[*Enter NATASHA.*]

NATASHA [*To the maid*]

What? Mr. Protopopov will sit with little Sophie, and Andrei can take little Bobik out. Children are such a bother ... [*To IRINA*] Irina, it's such a pity you're leaving to-morrow. Do stay one more week. [*Sees KULIGIN and screams; he laughs and takes off his false beard and whiskers*] You gave me such a fright! [*To IRINA*] I've grown used to you, do you think it'll be easy for me to see you go? I'm going to have Andrei and his violin put into your room – let him fiddle away in there! – and we'll put little Sophie into his room. Such a beautiful child! What a little darling! To-day she looked at me with such pretty eyes and said 'Mamma!'

KULIGIN

A beautiful child, it's quite true.

NATASHA

So I shall have the place to myself to-morrow. [*Sighs*] First I shall have that avenue of fir-trees cut down, then that maple. It's so ugly at nights ... [*To IRINA*] That sash doesn't suit you at all, dear ... It looks awful. And I'll have lots and lots of little flowers planted here, and they'll smell lovely ... [*Severely*] Why is there a fork lying about here on the bench? [*Going towards the house, to the maid*] Why is there a fork on the bench, I said? [*Shouts*] Don't you dare answer me back!

KULIGIN

Temper, temper! [*A march is played off; they all listen.*]

OLGA

They're going.

When, then, should you use emotion memory to help your acting? I'd suggest that you do so sparingly, when you are struggling to reach the level of emotional depth which you strongly suspect lies underneath a scene. It's very possible to skim along the surface of a play in rehearsal, resisting the urge to dive below and explore real emotional depths; after all, open displays of emotion can seem embarrassing, even in the rehearsal room. Part of your job as an actor is to sidestep such embarrassment and just 'go for it'. But how? Sitting in a circle remembering your own personal emotional lows (or highs) is surely very different from standing on a stage, trying to project real emotion while in character.

At its simplest there are two routes. You could try bringing all your imaginative powers to bear on the combined stimuli of the given circumstances, the 'want' you're fighting for, and the barriers which block the way. Or, you could find an emotionally charged situation in your own past which closely resembles the one your character currently finds themselves in, and then let your mind blend the two together into a single experience. This approach, which is usually referred to as 'substitution', can work really well – mainly because your audience can't read your mind, so they're happy to believe that your emotions belong to the character and not to you.

As with any attempt to generate real emotion, there are pitfalls. As an actor rehearsing or performing a play, you run the risk of starting to feel inadequate as, at each running of the unit, the repetition of the substituted memory starts to lose its intensity. Such fading is not only inevitable but also necessary – it's how we cope with grief in real life. You could try switching memories, finding something else that upsets you (if that's the emotion you're seeking). But how much fun is that? And what can it lead to? I once heard of an actor performing in a long run of a tragedy, who became so unhappy at losing the effects of his own sad memories that he started buying butterflies – which only live for one day – so that he could mourn each of their deaths nightly onstage. One day a Large Cabbage White failed to die on the appointed day and the actor, desperate for an experience to use, killed his own mother with a fencing foil.

Of course the story above is entirely made-up and utter nonsense (how many actors can afford to buy a butterfly every day?), but if you even for a moment believed the tale, then maybe that says more about the actor's dilemma than it does about your gullibility.

final thoughts

All actors, especially transformational character actors, need a reliable technique, if for no better reason than to have something to fall back on if the direction in the rehearsal room is unhelpful, if the character starts to become a caricature, or if spontaneity in performance starts to wane. But not everyone will want to approach acting in a structured way, such as the one offered in this book; you will need detective skills and a willingness to analyse, reflect and experiment. The 'Planning to Act' stage in particular can be hard work, though it really does pay dividends. Anyway, there it is: some tools, some practical techniques, some thoughts on how to be more versatile and more effective as an actor. Some of it, perhaps most of it, you will have encountered in some form elsewhere. But whether or not that's the case, I hope I have at least helped to keep the water clear in a pool which gets very clouded indeed; namely, how best to develop an actor's performance of a character.

Those who train student actors have a responsibility to empower them, to enable them to eventually function just as well, or better, without their teachers. Acting is a public activity, so actors in training need an audience to complete the essential triangle of 'A's which all theatre needs (Author, Actor and Audience). And public speaking, which is a massive part of acting in public, makes people nervous. So, whether you're using this book as a self-help guide, or working with a teacher, you really do need to practise doing what you do in front of a live audience. An actor who is unused to an audience can seem to resent their presence. That's disrespectful, and an audience feels it. If they like your perform-ance, you'll know, because, with practice, you'll sense it (well before the curtain call). But if an audience can't follow your communication – especially if they can't hear your words – one way or another, they'll tell you. That's another reason for the planning described in this book: if you're concentrating hard on your objective, and you're emotionally 'in role', then you're not worrying about what the person on the front row thinks of your acting.

In summary, then, here's how to deliver an excellent transformational character acting performance. Plan like an actor possessed. Experiment in rehearsal, and in private, with the vigour and playfulness of a young child. Then, on the day of performance, be properly warmed up, be appropriately 'in character' and 'in scene', and have a clear sense of the degree of vocal projection and diction required to reach the most distant audience member. Have confidence in all you've been doing to prepare; then go out and forget the detail – *all of it* – trusting, instead, to your skill as a spontaneous human being. And if you want to be really versatile as a transformational character actor, then remember – consciously at first, then unconsciously in performance – to:

use

t	(tension)
h	(height)
o	(openness)
s	(space)
e	(eye contact)
l	(loudness)
i	(inflection)
n	(note)
t	(tone)
p	(pace)
a	(accent)
d	(diction)
s	(specials)

appendix

Guidelines on filling in a Character Profile Sheet

Fill in a copy of the Character Profile Sheet on the next page each time you start work on a new character. Use a pencil so that you can make changes; you'll need a highlighter pen too.

Begin by sifting the script – you're looking for clues to your character. Then keep the sheet with you as rehearsals progress, adding and altering as you make new discoveries.

The sheet is in sections, and, once you've listed the key Facts down the left-hand side, the rest of the sheet can be completed in pretty well any order. Mostly it's self-explanatory, but below are some further guidelines which might help:

- *Favourite Fantasy:* this invites you to identify, or (when you know the character well enough) invent, a secret fantasy for your character. As well as helping you to add depth in understanding your character, this section also provides the basis for an interesting improvisation if time allows – this being, what would it feel like if your character's fantasy came true? If you were playing a servant who fantasises about being King, the experience of being served and lauded by everyone else in the story would be a powerful imagined memory.
- *Lifetime Objective:* this is an overarching 'want' which drives the character's overall behaviour at this point in his life. This is likely to be something which remains the same unless some massive incident impacts on your character's life to

NAME .... **Nickname** ....

Favourite Fantasy ....

FACTS
(include age, family, social position)

> *What you have heard others say about you*
>
> *(name the person who said it)*

LIFETIME OBJECTIVE:

"I want

PERSONALITY
(highlight your typical feelings and attitudes)

EXTRAVERT

sociable	easygoing	active	excitable
outgoing	lively	optimistic	aggressive
talkative	carefree	impulsive	restless
responsive	leader	changeable	touchy

STABLE — — — NEUROTIC

calm	peaceful	moody	pessimistic
even-tempered	thoughtful	anxious	reserved
reliable	passive	rigid	quiet
controlled	careful	sober	unsociable

INTROVERT

POWER	over whom?	describe it
Agreed		
Abuse		
Reward		
Information		
Connection		
Personal		

STATUS (key relationship)

Name of individual ....

STATUS SEESAW

My status   Their status

(draw in balance of status)

NAME Natasha **Nickname** Miss Bossyboots

from 'Three Sisters' by Chekhov

Favourite Fantasy Being guest of honour at a grand ball

FACTS

(include age, family, social position)

- local girl
- engaged to, then marries Andrei
- gains wealth through marriage
- runs the house once married
- becomes mother to Sophie and Bobik
- husband is would-be academic & gambler
- considered by some to have married above class
- learns French (Andrei's sisters speak other languages too)
- believes that servants should be sacked when too old to work at previous standard
- begins an affair with Protopopov

LIFETIME OBJECTIVE:

"I want to be accepted"

What you have heard others say about you

(name the person who said it)

"I love you – I want you to be my wife" – Andrei

"You're so young, so beautiful, so wonderful!" – Andrei

"You were so rude to Nanny just now" – Olga

"The way she's going around you'd think it was her who started the fire" – Masha

POSSIBLY OVERHEARD:

"It isn't Bobik that's sick, it's her up there...stupid woman" – Masha

"The way she dresses! – it's absolutely pitiful! And her cheeks shining, absolutely scrubbed! – Masha

PERSONALITY

(highlight your typical feelings and attitudes)

```
                      EXTRAVERT
        sociable    easygoing    active      excitable
        outgoing    lively       optimistic  (aggressive)
       (talkative)  carefree     (impulsive) restless
        responsive  leader       (changeable)(touchy)
STABLE ──────────────────────────────────────── NEUROTIC
            calm    peaceful     (moody)     pessimistic
    even-tempered   thoughtful   (anxious)   reserved
         reliable   passive      (rigid)     quiet
       controlled   careful      sober       (unsociable)
                      INTROVERT
```

POWER	over whom?	describe it
Agreed	the servants	orders them about
Abuse	the sisters & servants	loses her temper and threatens their rights*
Reward	Andrei and the children	gives them love and attention (and withdraws it)
Information	the sisters	she gains experience in raising children
Connection	the sisters/Andrei	gains higher social status through marriage
Personal	Andrei and Protopopov	considered very attractive

* has the power to sack Anfisa; demands that Irina give up her bedroom

STATUS (key relationship)

Name of individual .... Masha

STATUS SEESAW

My status   Their status

(draw in balance of status)

(feels socially inferior and feels Masha looks down on her)

change the lifetime objective. Examples are, 'to be famous', 'to help others', 'to do everything once before I die'.

- *Status Seesaw:* this section allows you to visualise your character's relationship with another, significant character in the script when the characters are first seen together. There is a thin 'plank' already drawn in on the seesaw; draw a new one which shows the balance of status between your character and the other person. The angle of the plank indicates, at a glance, the degree of relative status.

- *Nickname:* this is a useful 'aide-memoire' when acting a character, as a nickname is usually a potted descriptive label for a character's personality, whether it be 'Brains', 'Trouble', 'Sunshine' or whatever. Obviously nicknames which are simply words derived from a person's name rarely have any value in giving you a 'feel' for the character. In truth you'll probably need to make up the nickname; if this is the case, leave the nickname until last so that you have all the information you need to create a suitable one. And remember – we don't choose our own nicknames.

- *Personality Test:* use a highlighter pen to record the qualities, traits and attitudes which you confidently feel are shown by your character at some point in the play. The behaviour only has to be observed once. You'll almost certainly find interesting paradoxes and conflicts: a character may seem carefree one moment, pessimistic the next; peaceful here but restless two pages on. This section will help you to avoid stereotyping; like real people, well-written characters are complex creatures whose moods and thoughts can change radically, and without notice. And their behaviour may well alter in direct response to the company they keep. When you've filled in all the behaviours which your character shows in the play, you'll notice that there are more words highlighted in one 'quarter' of the diagram than in others. You can conclude from this whether your character is, on balance, say, a stable extrovert, or a neurotic introvert (or a different combination). This gives you a quick-reference sense of the personality of your character, and of how that personality differs from your own.

- *Power:* this is a quick-reference section to remind you of your character's power within key relationships. This section, brief though it is, can be crucial in affecting your character's behaviour towards others, since both he and the other person will normally be well aware of each other's power, and of the consequences of exercising that power. If other actors in the cast have completed this section too, there can be valuable discussion around power 'issues' in a play; if time allows, some valuable improvisation can also take place.

Relaxation Exercise with Visualisation

Wear loose, comfortable clothes. Remove shoes and lie flat on your back on a soft floor in a warm, quiet room. If you want to, you can tuck a soft pillow or something similar under your neck, and you can raise your knees up too if you find it more comfortable.

Shut your eyes and allow yourself to breathe at a normal pace and depth. Let your stomach rise and fall as you breathe.

Imagine that you're lying on a giant, strong, supportive, but soft sponge. The muscle tension in your body is something which you want to be rid of; visualise it as a coloured liquid or gel which will sink down into the sponge if you let it.

Start by tensing your toes. Imagine that your feet are claws, toes curled downwards. Hold this position for a count of ten, then relax: as you relax, visualise the tension which you were holding in your toes draining away into the sponge below you.

Now curl your toes upwards. Visualise the tension held in your muscles. After counting silently to ten, relax, letting the tension drain away into the sponge below you.

Work systematically through your body in this way, tensing and relaxing the muscles in this order: your ankles; legs below the knee; the knees; the thighs; bottom; lower back; stomach; upper back; chest; shoulders; hands (make them into tight fists, then spread your fingers wide as if you have webbed hands); wrists; forearms; elbows; upper arms; shoulders again; neck (tense only gently); face (make your face as small as you possibly can, then spread your features as wide as you can).

When everything has been tensed and relaxed, make a mental check of whether any tension has crept back in. If you think it may have, mentally isolate that part of your body and repeat the exercise with the visualisation.

As you lie there, try to remember just how this state of being fully relaxed feels.

In your own time, slowly raise yourself up from this relaxed state, so that you are standing. Be conscious of using only the muscles which are necessary for standing.

Accents scrapbook: an example

Here's an example of a possible scrapbook entry for the **Liverpool accent**:

Loudness – no specific trait, can be loud or soft or in between. The caricature scouser speaks loudly, but in reality there are plenty of quiet scouse voices.

Inflection – scouse has a definite and recognisable inflection pattern, which tends to have repeating patterns. The inflection pattern is often confused with that of the Birmingham accent, but there are subtle differences. Scousers tend to use a narrower-than-normal range of notes in normal speech, and sentences often end with an upward inflection.

Note – no specific trait, other than that male speakers can tend towards use of higher notes as part of the exciteable quality of this urban accent.

Tone – tends to be hard, caused by some tension towards the back of the throat and on the soft palate (on the roof of the mouth nearer the throat).

Pace – tends to be fast, part of the speaker's identity for being quick-witted. But individual words can habitually glide into the 'er' sound to allow the speaker thinking time, such as 'so – er'.

Diction – tends to be fairly poor, caused in part by habitual limited use of the mouth and lips to form words. There's a 'splashiness' to certain sounds – the word 'hat' can come out as almost 'hats', with a soft 't'. 'Great' can sound almost like 'grace'. The hard 'c' and 'k' sounds can sound splashy at the end of a word, so that 'kick' can sound like 'kikh', with the hard sound at the end of the word being held momentarily on the soft palate.

Specials – thick 's' sounds are common, often as a result of only limited use of the tongue during speech. The tongue may protrude minutely through the teeth.

Words: certain words are substituted when compared with Standard English. 'We did it' may come out as 'we done it'; 'we didn't' can become 'we never'.

Famous speakers: the Beatles; recent example: footballer Steven Gerrard.

Recorded examples:
http://www.collectbritain.co.uk/personalisation/object.cfm?uid=021MMC900S10055U00002C01 (interview with older male scouser)
http://www.collectbritain.co.uk/personalisation/object.cfm?uid=021MMC900S10010U00001C01 (interview with older female scouser)
http://www.ku.edu/~idea/europe/england/england16.mp3
(younger male Scouser reading a story)

Further Reading

Actor's Guide to Getting Work – Simon Dunmore (A & C Black)

An Actor Prepares – Konstantin Stanislavski (Methuen)

Building a Character – Konstantin Stanislavski (Methuen)

Clear Speech – Malcolm Morrison (A & C Black)

Confusions: Acting Edition S. – Alan Ayckbourn (Samuel French Ltd)

English Phonetics and Phonology: A Practical Course – Peter Roach (Cambridge University Press)

Impro: Improvisation and the Theatre – Keith Johnstone (Methuen)

In the Company of Actors – Carole Zucker (A & C Black)

John Godber Plays: Bouncers, Happy Families, Shakers – John Godber (Methuen)

Mindwatching – Hans and Michael Eysenck (Book Club Associates)

NLP at Work – Sue Knight (Nicholas Brealey Publishing)

The Pocket Guide to Manwatching – Desmond Morris (Triad Books)

Talking for Britain – Simon Elmes (Penguin Reference)

True and False: Heresy and Common Sense for the Actor – David Mamet (Faber and Faber)

Voice and Speech in the Theatre – Malcolm Morrison and Clifford Turner (A & C Black)

Voice and the Actor – Cicely Berry (Virgin Books)

Official website for H J Eysenck: http://freespace.virgin.net/darrin.evans

Official website for the author: www.paulelsam.com

glossary

Abuse power is power which a person uses to force another person to do something (e.g. a school bully threatens to hurt another child unless money is handed over). Abuse power is also used when a person with Agreed power abuses their authority (e.g. a doctor inappropriately asks a patient to strip).

Accent is a characteristic of voice and speech which reveals where you are likely to have been brought up, and/or which social class you belong to. Each regional accent can be deconstructed to assess its typical characteristics, using the criteria of Loudness, Inflection, Note, Tone, Pace, Diction and 'Specials'.

Agreed power is power which a person is allowed to use as a result of his position within a culture (e.g. a manager can ask a junior member of a team to carry out a duty; a police officer is allowed to arrest a suspect; a parent can stop a child's pocket money as a punishment).

Ayckbourn, Sir Alan is Artistic Director of the Stephen Joseph Theatre in Scarborough, and the world's most widely performed living playwright. He writes plays for adult audiences (including *Confusions*, *Season's Greetings*, *The Norman Conquests* and *Joking Apart*), and for family audiences (including *My Very Own Story* and *The Champion of Paribanou*). Musicals include *By Jeeves* with Andrew Lloyd Webber and *Dreams from a Summer House* with John Pattison.

Beckett, Samuel was an Irish-born Nobel Prize-winning absurdist playwright whose theatre experiments ranged from *Waiting for Godot* – in which two tramps wait for someone called Godot who never arrives – to *Not I*, in which the only thing seen is the carefully lit mouth of the solo actor. Often writing in French, Beckett's other plays include *Endgame*, *Krapps's Last Tape* and *Happy Days*.

Berkoff, Steven is a controversial London-born playwright, director and actor whose highly stylised plays include *East*, *West*, *Decadence*, *Sink the Belgrano* and *Messiah*. Adaptations include Kafka's *The Trial* and Edgar Allan Poe's *The Fall of the House of Usher*. Berkoff has also worked widely on screen, often playing a villain in films such as *Octopussy* and *Beverly Hills Cop*.

Character actor is a term most often used to describe an older actor who makes his or her living portraying one key character 'type' – e.g. 'tough guy', 'grumpy old woman'. In films their character is often a supporting character to the lead actor(s), so there are few really famous character actors. In the UK, actors such as Steven Berkoff and Annette Badlands are perhaps better-known examples.

Character Profile Sheet offers a method, devised by the author of this book, for ensuring that actors gain sufficient relevant information on a character before and during rehearsal. The single-page sheet requires actors to read a script carefully and record any salient information. The actor can then fill in any gaps using his developing awareness and his knowledge of the character.

Chekhov, Michael was a Russian-born teacher, actor, director and theorist and former student of Stanislavski. He left Russia for England, where he founded an Acting Studio which later relocated to the United States. His experimental work with actors led to the development of new approaches to acting, which were partially eclipsed in the USA by 'The Method'.

Classicist actors are drawn to text which is filled with imagery, and which is challenging to deliver. They enjoy a sense of comfort with the textual style of 'the classics'. At best, they combine the skills of the Inhabiter and the Storyteller to tell a character's story truthfully. At worst, they can overindulge in the poetry of the text. Their skill combines the best of the other two types, but adds a sense of fearlessness towards 'difficult' text.

Connection power is power which comes from being close to someone who has power (e.g. a school pupil is the daughter of the headmaster; you have a friend who is a famous film actor).

Diction means clarity of speech. Clear speech, which is essential for actors, is achieved mainly through a combination of active use of the muscles involved in speech – mainly the lips – and through a relaxed, yet energised, ability to project your voice effectively, including projection of the sounds made when vowels are used in speech.

Dipthong occurs when one verb sound slides into another, with no consonant in between. The word 'boy' is an example of a particularly strong dipthong, which, in standard English, slides from the sound which you get in the middle of the word 'good', to the sound that you get in the middle of the word 'hit'. Short words such as 'go' are dipthongs, as are 'may' and 'hear'. Dipthong sounds often vary greatly from accent to accent.

Emotion memory describes a rehearsal and performance activity in which an actor tackles a moment in the story of his character, by imaginatively provoking himself with memories of analogous situations from his own life. Ideally the revisiting of an emotional experience from the actor's own life will be 'read' by the audience as a true emotional response of the character to the story.

Eye contact describes how we use our eyes to observe things, and to 'read' other people. We also use it to signal or disguise our own feelings and intentions. The direction, and the duration, of eye contact between people is significant. Continuous eye contact ('staring'), no eye contact, and 'flickered' eye contact (when people look up briefly then quickly look away) are all significant in revealing a person's confidence, and their sense of relative status.

Eysenck, Hans – the late psychologist, researcher and writer whose substantial body of work includes *Mindwatching* and *Know Your Own Personality*. See Further Reading for a link to the Eysenck website.

Glottal stop is a characteristic of voice and speech in which voiced outward breath is momentarily trapped in the throat. Common to accents such as London cockney and Newcastle geordie, the glottal stop acts as a substitute for a consonant in a word or phrase – usually the 't' sound – so that 'bottle' becomes 'bo'l'.

Godber, John is a playwright and Artistic Director of Hull Truck Theatre in Hull, East Yorkshire. Plays include *Bouncers*, *Up 'n' Under*, *Teechers* and *Shakers* (co-written with Jane Thornton). Musicals include *Thick as a Brick* and the family musical *Big Trouble in the Little Bedroom* (both with John Pattison).

Gogol, Nickolai was a Russian writer whose works include *The Government Inspector* (1836) – recently revived in adapted form at the National Theatre in London as *The UN Inspector* – and the novel *Dead Souls*.

Height describes, for the purposes of this book, a person's manipulated height, as compared to their 'natural' height. The reasons why they manipulate their height so that it differs from their natural height may be straightforward (e.g. they sit because they are tired), or psychologically significant (e.g. they sit because they are acknowledging their lower status compared to another person who stands).

Humanimal is another word for the human animal. The author uses the term as a way of reminding the reader that, beneath our sophisticated veneer, we are still animals – with all the basic urges and needs that go with that condition. For instance, while most humans no longer hunt for their own food, they do still fight for status and power in society.

Inflection describes the way in which we move through different notes when using our voices. We alter inflection to add meaning: it helps the listener to understand what we are saying, and to prioritise the importance of the different words we speak. Inflection is also used to express feeling, for example through a yawn, or through laughter. The degree of inflection a person uses can reveal significant things about their state of mind.

Inhabiter actors need to 'become' a character. They work hard to engage psychologically and emotionally with the circumstances within a character's story. At best they can be deeply moving for an audience to observe; at worst, they can be resentful of an audience's presence, which can hamper their technique.

Inner life refers to the psychological and emotional activity in which an actor is involved during rehearsal and performance. Sometimes this inner activity will be clearly expressed through spontaneous non-verbal behaviour; at other times an audience will unconsciously sense, perhaps through some emotional quality in an actor's voice, that the actor is experiencing intense thought and feeling.

Johnstone, Keith is a teacher, writer and director who has pioneered techniques for improvisation, initially through his work at the Royal Court Theatre in London. Currently a professor at the University of Calgary in Canada, he is co-founder of the Loose Moose theatre company, and has written the books *Impro* and *Impro for Storytellers*.

Knowledge power is power which comes from having information or expertise that is needed by someone else (e.g. a homeless person knows the location of the nearest taxi rank; a technician is able to repair a computer problem).

Labelling is the process by which a person's sense of identity alters as a result of the way they are treated by others. So a person who is regarded by others as having 'no common sense' may well start to share that belief. Their altered belief then translates into altered behaviour, so that they may for example become less confident and more indecisive.

Loudness refers to vocal loudness or volume, which can reveal important psychological things about a person. Confident people are often loud; shy people are often quiet. Vocal volume becomes interesting when people's preferred volume is inappropriate; when a shy person is public speaking, for example. People may also manipulate their volume for effect: the super-confident person trying to attract a shy person may adopt a quieter, more intimate vocal level.

Lifetime objective is an overarching 'want' which drives a character's overall behaviour. This is likely to be something which remains the same unless some massive incident impacts on the character's life to change the lifetime objective. Examples are, 'to be famous', 'to help others', 'to do everything once before I die'.

Magic what if? refers to Stanislavski's idea that convincing, truthful acting needs to be provoked imaginatively. Any situation faced by a character in a play can be explored using an empathetic imaginative approach in which the actor places himself in that imagined situation, and responds spontaneously to it.

Mamet, David is an American playwright, director and screenwriter whose plays include *Oleanna, The Duck Variations, Sexual Perversity in Chicago*, and *American Buffalo*. He was awarded the

Pulitzer Prize in 1984 for *Glengarry Glen Ross*. Books include *True and False*.

Method acting is a phrase most often used to refer to the style of acting which demands that an actor should always experience, and re-experience, true, spontaneous emotion during performance. Adapted from the teachings of Stanislavski, 'The Method' is credited most of all to the American actor, teacher and director Lee Strasberg.

Miller, Arthur was a Pulitzer Prize-winning American playwright whose plays include *The Crucible*, *All My Sons*, *A View from the Bridge* and *Death of a Salesman*. His plays continued to be performed even after his blacklisting by the House of UnAmerican Activities Committee. After the Hollywood Blacklist was lifted, Miller wrote the screenplay for the film *The Misfits*.

Note describes the individual sound which combines with other sounds to form Inflection. Unlike in singing or in music, a vocal note is never in- or out-of-tune, since the voice spontaneously uses an infinitely wide range of notes, including the areas 'between' notes on the traditional musical scale.

Objective is a term which describes what a character is fighting to achieve at any given moment in a scene. When a script has been divided into units, the actor views each unit from his character's perspective and tries to work out what the character is trying to achieve in relation to others. Each discrete 'want' becomes the character's specific objective in each unit. Examples of playable objectives include 'I want to make you smile' and 'I want you to leave the room'.

Olivier, Laurence was a British-born Oscar-winning transformational character actor and co-founder of the National Theatre in London, who performed widely on the stage as well as on screen. Films include *Rebecca*, *Wuthering Heights*, *The Marathon Man* and Shakespeare's *Henry V*. He became Lord Olivier in 1971.

Openness describes the degree to which we open up or conceal the front of the body. When standing, 'fully open' means legs apart, head raised, arms away from torso (e.g. hands on hips); while 'fully closed' means legs entwined, head tilted down, arms folded tightly across chest or stomach. The degree of openness is one of the most influential bodily signs; you can make a strong initial judgement on a person's state of mind by looking at their openness from some distance away. The ultimate degree of concealment and self-protection is the foetal position.

Pace describes the speed at which speech takes place. As with most personal characteristics, speed of speech creates different perceptions of the speaker. Fast speech can suggest confidence, quick-wittedness, spontaneity, energy. Slow speech can suggest reticence, low intelligence, cautiousness, listlessness. But fast speech can also suggest nervousness; and slow speech can be the sign of a confident person who chooses to dictate the pace of communication.

Personal power is power which comes from a person's attractiveness to others, either because of their looks, or their personality (e.g. a model, or a member of a group who can tell jokes brilliantly).

Phonetic alphabet is the alphabet of sounds which experts use to deconstruct speech. The phonetic alphabet can be invaluable in helping actors to master accents; but the actor must be willing to learn a wide range of symbols from this alphabet, and will need a good 'ear' to hear the subtle differences between sounds in any given accent.

Physical barrier is a practical obstruction which limits a character's ability to achieve an objective. If the objective is, 'I want to know if you were lying', physical barriers might be, 'but I can't see your eyes behind your sunglasses', or 'I can't hear your tone of voice well enough over the noise from traffic'.

Physical status is a term used to describe how a person's non-verbal behaviour automatically claims a position for them on the status 'seesaw'. Tension, height, openness, use of space, and eye contact ('THOSE') can all be altered to claim a lower or higher position in relation to another person.

Pinter, Harold is a Nobel Prize-winning playwright, director and actor whose plays include *The Birthday Party*, *The Caretaker*, *Betrayal*, *One for the Road* and *The Hothouse*. Screenplays include *The Go-Between* and *The French Lieutenant's Woman*.

Psychological barrier is a thought or feeling which makes it more difficult for a character to achieve the objective they are fighting for. If the objective is, 'I want to kiss you', psychological barriers might be, say, 'but I'm not sure you find me attractive', or 'but I'm married'.

Relaxation means shedding the body of as much unnecessary muscular tension as possible. Actors often put themselves through a structured relaxation prior to performance (see 'Relaxation Exercise with Visualisation' in the Appendix), to help them feel focused and in control, and to help them build the physical profile of their character.

Representational acting is now mostly used as a term of disparagement to describe an outdated style of acting in which stylised movement and poetical vocal delivery was preferred over spontaneous, emotional truthfulness. The performances in the early to mid-20th century by English actors such as the young John Gielgud and Noel Coward stand as examples. Latterly the term has been used to describe actors whose skilful perform-ances do not require the actor to experience constant emotion.

Resonators are chambers of varying size which are situated throughout the upper body. They include the mouth, nose, throat and lungs, and also the sinuses – tiny chambers peppered around the skull. Each of these resonators has the potential to help the voice to be amplified, and to enhance tone.

Reward power describes the power to supply something which is valued by another person (e.g. an interviewer rewards a candidate with a job; a parent rewards a child with a sweet; a child rewards a parent with a smile).

Russell, Willy is a Liverpool-born playwright whose stage plays include *Our Day Out, Stags and Hens, Shirley Valentine* and *Educating Rita* (the last two were also made into films). He also wrote the book, words and music for the musical, *Blood Brothers*.

Seesaw principle refers to Keith Johnstone's stated rule-of-thumb which dictates that the raising of a person's status will always simultaneously lower the status of someone, or something, else; and vice versa.

Sellers, Peter was an acclaimed British transformational character actor whose films include *Being There, I'm Alright Jack* and the *Pink Panther* series. In the Stanley Kubrick film *Doctor Strangelove* he convincingly portrayed three wildly differing central characters.

Sense memory describes a rehearsal and performance activity in which an actor achieves a sense of truthfulness during a moment in the story of his character, by provoking himself with memories of analogous situations from his own life in which some combination of the five senses was intensely experienced. Ideally the revisiting of a sensory memory from the actor's own life will add authenticity to the actor's performance.

Shakespeare, William was an English-born Elizabethan playwright and actor whose works between 1588 and 1616 include *Hamlet, King Lear, The Tempest, Comedy of Errors* and *A Midsummer Night's Dream*. He is also known for his prolific output of Sonnets.

Showreel is a videotape, DVD or website address which showcases the previous work of an actor for the benefit of casting directors, agents and directors. This will normally be edited to feature only scenes from productions in which the actor appears, and ideally will contain only professional work in which the actor can be viewed performing dialogue.

Social status attaches to a person as a result of how society views people in their position. In this hierarchy a queen is deemed more important than a bank manager, but the bank manager has higher social status than an office cleaner, who has higher social status than someone who is long-term unemployed. Your 'normal' social status is always lurking there in the background when people interact with you, and it has much to do with power: the more power you have to influence others, the higher up the social hierarchy you will be.

Space is the area surrounding your body which you use, or decide not to use. In this book we are concerned with how you move within space when other people are nearby – how much, or how little, physical space you claim. It can be visualised as a flexible invisible bubble which each person carries with them. People claim space through their bodily size and movement, and through their attitude; so to understand space in relation to bodies you need to be familiar with the other four characteristics of movement – tension, height, openness, and eye contact. All four variables allow you to claim or abandon the space which another person might want.

Specials are common idiosyncrasies of speech. They include substitution of the sounds 'f' for 'th' ('fink' instead of 'think');

difficulty pronouncing the strong 'r' (so that 'worry' becomes 'wowy'); mispronunciation of the 's' sound to produce something like a 'th' ('thith-ter' instead of 'sister'); and the glottal stop.

Spontaneity is an important goal for all actors. It represents the achievement of the act of imaginatively living 'in the moment' during a performance. Achieving spontaneity brings with it an ease which enables the actor, and his fellow actors, to make correct and truthful choices during performance. If all actors in a scene are achieving spontaneity, the performance will seem to 'light up' emotionally. However the actors must remember to maintain good technique (e.g. voice projection) even while achieving imaginative spontaneity.

Spotlight is the directory of actors' photographs which is published annually. The publication is aimed at (and issued to) directors and casting directors, to help them with the casting process. Spotlight is published online as well as in print.

Standard English is a supposedly 'neutral' accent used by some speakers in the UK, which comprises sounds which are not specific to any particular regional accent. Once common to broadcasters and actors (and referred to as 'BBC English'), the accent nowadays may identify the speaker as being middle, or upper middle, class.

Stanislavski, Konstantin was a Russian-born actor, director, writer and theorist who developed the first systematic approach to naturalistic acting in the early 20th century. Books include *An Actor Prepares*, *Being a Character*, *My Life in Art*. His influence on acting in the West remains strong to this day.

Storyteller actors enjoy telling the story of the play to the audience. Communication is focused primarily on this task, and even if actors never actually look at the audience they are always aware of them, reaching through the divide to share a character's experience. From the audience's perspective the Storyteller can be a hugely entertaining performer; at worst, he can lack engagement with his fellow actors, and can lack truth.

Strasberg, Lee was an American teacher, actor, director and theorist whose work with former students of Stanislavski led to the formation of the New York-based Acting Studio, and the development of the American Method (or 'The Method') approach to acting.

Subtext describes the thoughts and motivations which lay behind the words spoken by a character. Modern playwrights almost always disguise some of their characters' true thoughts and intentions, in order to achieve a sense of psychological realism. Actors need to be sensitised to this.

Tension is a word to describe the presence of tensed muscles in the body. At any given moment muscles are tightened, or relaxed. The amount of tension, and the degree to which muscles are tensed when it is not physically essential, reveals something significant about the psychological state of the individual.

Tone describes the degree of 'hardness' or 'softness' in the quality of a person's voice. It is altered as a result of three key factors in the body: how relaxed the muscles are around the voice-amplifying resonators; how freely the breath flows during speech; and where the note is pitched. These three factors are interrelated, so that a soft tone will typically occur if a low note is used to breathe freely through a relaxed upper body.

Transactional analysis is a theory in which verbal status behaviour falls into one of three types: adult, parent, or child. It is suggested that in speech we unconsciously select one of these roles to communicate; and that we often choose a role which is at odds with our social status. A parent might spontaneously adopt child behaviour by losing emotional control and 'throwing a tantrum'; the same person, at work as a teacher, might nurture an adult-to-adult way of working with students.

Transformational character actor is an actor who is skilled in greatly altering physical and vocal characteristics to enable him or her to 'inhabit' a range of characters. Examples include Peter Sellers, Daniel Day Lewis, Meryl Streep, Sir Ben Kingsley.

True root note is the natural vocal note which you make when you're fully relaxed, for example when you vocalise a yawn in private. People have different root notes, both for physiological reasons (determined mainly by size and tension within the vocal cords) and psychological reasons (when people become socialised into behaving in ways other people expect them to behave – a woman adopting a higher root note to appeal to men, for example – giving rise to a public root note).

Unit is a term used to describe a small (perhaps half a page) section of script in which each of the characters in a scene is engaged in a single significant objective or 'want'. When there is a change in circumstances – e.g. a character in the story enters or leaves, or one character starts to push for something new within the scene – that unit ends and the next one begins.

Verbal status is a term used to describe how a speaker's choice of words, and the attitude behind those words, automatically claim a position for the speaker on the status 'seesaw'. If two people on the imaginary seesaw have opposite social status – a queen and a tramp, for example – then verbal status activity can instantly undermine the established relative social status and so change the overall status balance. Higher status can be claimed either by lowering that of the other person (e.g. by insulting them), or by raising your own (e.g. by praising yourself).

Visualisation is the technique of harnessing the imagination to mentally 'see' something happen. Visualisation is used to build self-confidence, or to prepare for an experience. For an actor this might mean anything from using visualisation to improve relaxation skill (see 'Relaxation Exercise with Visualisation' in the Appendix), to visualising an intense and significant 'in-character' moment which occurs away from the script.

index